Mapping the Landscape

Mapping the Landscape: Explorations in Psychoanalysis offers an overview and exploration of Priscilla Roth's unique contribution to psychoanalysis over the course of her long and distinguished career.

This book takes the reader on a journey through psychoanalytic clinical practice and the significance of themes such as identity, identification, idealization and reparation. This collection shows a variety of Roth's interests but also the continuity of her approach – the unconscious thread, which links thoughts and memories together. Through close examination of the moment-to-moment psychoanalytic work, she emphasizes how unconscious processes influence both patient and analyst without either of them becoming aware of it. In this sense, each analysis is unique. The second part of the book allows for reflection on lessons drawn from her work, and how psychoanalysis poses the question of what it means to be oneself for the analyst and the patient.

Reflecting her strong compassion for patients and depth of understanding of the nature of psychoanalysis, this is key reading for psychoanalysts, psychotherapists and anyone interested in the experiences underpinning humanity in each of us.

Priscilla Roth is a training and supervising analyst at the Institute of Psychoanalysis, where she was head of training. Following her degree in psychology and working as a research assistant at the University of California, Berkeley, she trained as a child and adolescent psychotherapist at the Tavistock Clinic, and an analyst with the British Psychoanalytical Society. She has lectured at both institutions, the University College London, and internationally. She had been elected as a Distinguished Fellow of the British Psychoanalytical Society in 2022. She published many papers and edited several books, including *Imaginary Existences: A Psychoanalytic Exploration of Phantasy, Fiction, Dreams and Daydreams*, by Ignês Sodré, and *Envy and Gratitude Revisited*.

Ignês Sodré is a training and supervising analyst of the British Psychoanalytical Society. She has taught extensively in London and abroad, and was the first visiting professorial fellow in psychoanalysis at Birkbeck College. She has published on psychoanalysis and on literature, and authored *Imaginary Existences: A Psychoanalytic Exploration of Phantasy, Fiction, Dreams and Daydreams*.

Tomasz Fortuna is a psychoanalyst with the British Psychoanalytical Society. He works at the Portman Clinic and in private practice in London. He was a visiting professor in psychoanalysis at the University Putra Malaysia and co-authored *Melanie Klein: The Basics*.

The New Library of Psychoanalysis

General Editor: Anne Patterson

The *New Library of Psychoanalysis* is published by Routledge Mental Health in association with the *Institute of Psychoanalysis*, London.

The purpose of the book series is:

- to advance and disseminate ideas in psychoanalysis amongst those working in psychoanalysis, psychotherapy and related fields
- to facilitate a greater and more widespread appreciation of psychoanalysis in the general book-reading public
- to provide a forum for increasing mutual understanding between psychoanalysts and those in other disciplines
- to facilitate communication between different traditions and cultures within psychoanalysis, making some of the work of continental and other non-English speaking analysts more readily available to English-speaking readers, and increasing the interchange of ideas between British and American analysts.

The *New Library of Psychoanalysis* published its first book in 1987 under the editorship of David Tuckett, who was followed by Elizabeth Bott Spillius, Susan Budd, Dana Birksted-Breen and Alessandra Lemma. The Editors, including the current Editor, Anne Patterson, have been assisted by a considerable number of Associate Editors and readers from a range of countries and psychoanalytic traditions. **The present Associate Editors are Susanne Calice, Katalin Lanczi and Anna Streeruwitz.**

Under the guidance of Foreign Rights Editors, a considerable number of the *New Library* books have been published abroad, particularly in Brazil, Germany, France, Italy, Peru, Spain and Japan. The *New Library of Psychoanalysis* has also translated and published several books by continental psychoanalysts and plans to continue the policy of publishing books that express as clearly as possible a variety of psychoanalytic points of view. The *New Library of Psychoanalysis* has published books representing all three schools of thought in British psychoanalysis, including a particularly important work edited by Pearl King and Riccardo Steiner, 'The Freud-Klein Controversies 1941–45', expounding the intellectual and organisational controversies that

'Reading Priscilla Roth's papers, collected here for the first time, is a remarkable pleasure: lucid, compassionate and deeply humane, she brings the reader into the consulting room where we follow her careful thinking alongside her experience of her patients. These richly attuned, precisely depicted essays bring psychoanalysis to life. Singularly adept at evoking the texture of an analytic hour, Roth conveys complex theoretical principles in language every analyst will appreciate.'

Dr. Lynne Zeavin, *The New York Psychoanalytic Society & Institute, Journal of American Psychoanalytic Association*

'*Mapping the Landscape* shows us a skillful clinician and lucid psychoanalytic thinker at work. Priscilla Roth's essays are important contributions to contemporary Kleinian literature. They are already required reading on various clinical trainings, and, thanks to this book, will deservedly gain a still wider readership. Highly recommended.'

Prof. Daniel Pick, *Birkbeck, University of London, and British Psychoanalytical Society*

'This collection of Priscilla Roth's papers over a lifetime of practice as a distinguished psychoanalyst is prefaced and introduced by lucid contributions by John Steiner, Tomasz Fortuna and Ignes Sodre. These papers by Priscilla Roth are stimulating, insightful and the evidence of an intelligent mind at work on the human condition. We are given access to the very convincing process of her thinking and finding ways to communicate with her patients that is illuminating for all of us working in this field. We highly recommend this interesting and intelligent book.'

Martha Papadakis and **Ron Britton**, *British Psychoanalytical Society*

'This is a fine collection of psychoanalytic papers, which reflects Priscilla Roth's clinical experience and knowledge, and the deep understanding and sympathy with her patients. The writing is clear and direct, and she has the capacity to make even complex ideas accessible to her reader. This book should be of great interest and value to a wide variety of readers.'

Michael Feldman, *Distinguished Fellow, British Psychoanalytical Society*

developed in the British psychoanalytical Society between Kleinian, Viennese and 'middle group' analysts during the Second World War.

The *New Library of Psychoanalysis* aims for excellence in psychoanalytic publishing. Submitted manuscripts are rigorously peer-reviewed in order to ensure high standards of scholarship, clinical communications, and writing.

For a full list of all the titles in the New Library of Psychoanalysis main series as well as both the New Library of Psychoanalysis 'Teaching Series' and 'Beyond the Couch' subseries, please visit the Routledge website.

Mapping the Landscape
Explorations in Psychoanalysis

Priscilla Roth

Edited by
Ignês Sodré and Tomasz Fortuna

Routledge
Taylor & Francis Group

LONDON AND NEW YORK

Designed cover image: © Nicholas Garland

First published 2026
by Routledge
4 Park Square, Milton Park, Abingdon, Oxon OX14 4RN

and by Routledge
605 Third Avenue, New York, NY 10158

Routledge is an imprint of the Taylor & Francis Group, an informa business

© 2026 Priscilla Roth

British Library Cataloguing-in-Publication Data
A catalogue record for this book is available from the British Library

ISBN: 978-1-032-96274-0 (hbk)
ISBN: 978-1-032-95947-4 (pbk)
ISBN: 978-1-003-58887-0 (ebk)

DOI: 10.4324/9781003588870

Typeset in Optima
by Taylor & Francis Books

For Nick

Contents

PART II
Lectures and Essay

Acknowledgements

First of all I must thank my editors, Ignês Sodré and Tomasz Fortuna, for their careful and dedicated work throughout the process of preparing this book for publication. My thanks also to Anne Patterson, series editor of the New Library of Psychoanalysis, who was supportive and helpful from the beginning of the project.

I am grateful to my colleagues at the Betty Joseph Workshop for many years of discussing our clinical work together; and to Ron Britton, Michael Feldman and John Steiner for the experience of the West Lodge Conferences.

John Steiner read and made helpful comments on several versions of the chapters in this book. His work and advice have been invaluable over many years; equally important to me is our close friendship. Ignês Sodré and I discussed all our work together since we were young analysts; I am very grateful for all her help in making this book possible. It is difficult to convey in words the depth of gratitude that I feel towards my analyst Leslie Sohn.

Because they were never far from my mind, and each played a part in shaping my work, I want to acknowledge first my parents, Bernard and Elaine Brandchaft; also, my late husband Anthony Roth, who was with me, and helped me throughout my training and the earliest days of my professional life as a psychoanalyst, and was the father of my sons Gabriel and Zachary.

This book is for Nick, with all my gratitude.

It is a sad duty to mention the tragic death of Ignês Sodré while the book was nearing completion.

The following kindly gave permission to use previously published material:

- Chapter 1: Roth, P. (2001) Mapping The Landscape: Levels of Transference Interpretation. *International Journal of Psychoanalysis* 82: 533–543.
- Chapter 3: Roth, P. (1994) Being True to a False Object: A View of Identification. *Psychoanalytic Inquiry* 14: 393–405.
- Chapter 4: Roth, P. (1999) Absolute Zero: A Man Who Doubts His Own Love … *International Journal of Psychoanalysis* 80: 661–670.
- Chapter 5: Roth, P. (2018) 'I Used to Think You Were Wonderful': The Persecution/Idealisation Cycle of Melancholia. In P. Garvey and K. Long (eds), *The Klein Tradition: Lines of Development: Evolution of Theory*

and *Practice over the Decades*. London: Routledge. The clinical material in this chapter was originally published in by L. Glocer Fiorini, T. Bokanowski and S. Lewkowicz (eds), *On Freud's 'Mourning and Melancholia'*. London: International Psychoanalytical Association.

- Chapter 10: Roth, P. (2008) Introduction. In P. Roth and A. Lemma (eds), *Envy and Gratitude Revisited*. London: Routledge.

About the Author and Editors

Priscilla Roth is a training and supervising analyst at the British Institute of Psychoanalysis, where she was head of the training. She was born in New Orleans in the United States and grew up in Los Angeles. Following her degree in psychology at the University of California at the Berkeley, she continued her research there and in Massachusetts. After she came to London in the early 1970s, she trained first as a child and adolescent psychotherapist at the Tavistock Clinic, and shortly thereafter as an adult analyst with the British Psychoanalytical Society. She has lectured at both institutions, and the University College London. She has taught in Britain and internationally in Europe and the United States, and had been elected as a Distinguished Fellow of the British Psychoanalytical Society in 2022. Her clinical work illustrates a profound understanding of the complex interplay between the impact of early developmental experiences and the role of unconscious phantasy in shaping the development of the mind. She is the author of a large number of papers and chapters and the editor of several books, including, *On Bearing Unbearable States of Mind: the work of Ruth Malcolm* and, with Richard Rusbridger, *Encounters with Melanie Klein: Selected Papers of Elizabeth Spillius*, and most recently, *Imaginary Existences: A Psychoanalytic Exploration of Phantasy, Fiction, Dreams and Daydreams*, by Ignês Sodré; and, with Alessandra Lemma, *Envy and Gratitude Revisited.*

Ignês Sodré is a training and supervising analyst of the British Psychoanalytical Society. She was born in Brazil, where she qualified as a clinical psychologist before moving to London in 1969 to train at the Institute of Psychoanalysis. She has scholarly knowledge of, and a profound interest in, both psychoanalysis and literature, and a unique and creative way of linking psychoanalysis and literature, which enriches both fields. She has taught extensively in London and abroad, and was the first visiting professorial Fellow in Psychoanalysis at Birkbeck College. She has published many papers on psychoanalysis and on literature; co-authored a book with A. S. Byatt, *Imagining Characters: Six Conversations about Women Writers*, and authored, *Imaginary Existences: A Psychoanalytic Exploration of Phantasy;*

Fiction, Dreams and Daydreams. As mentioned above, Ignês Sodré tragically died after editing of this book was completed.

Tomasz Fortuna is a psychoanalyst with the British Psychoanalytical Society and a founding-member of the Hanna Segal Institute for Psychoanalytic Studies. He worked as a psychiatrist in the NHS for 16 years and now at the Portman Clinic and in private psychoanalytic practice. He teaches and supervises at the Tavistock and Portman Clinics, Institute of Psychoanalysis, University College London and abroad, and was a Visiting Professor in Psychoanalysis at the psychiatry department of University Putra Malaysia. His professional interests include the relationship between psychoanalysis and the arts, and the understanding of severe emotional disturbance and criminal behaviour. He published several articles and chapters, co-authored with R. D. Hinshelwood, *Melanie Klein: The Basics* and edited, *Bion's Vertices: On Truth and Lies.*

Preface

John Steiner

This volume confirms Priscilla Roth's position as a leading contributor to contemporary Kleinian psychoanalysis. It shows the influence of her American background as well as the analytic training she acquired during her life in London. She was born in New Orleans in 1943 and grew up in Los Angeles where her mother, Elaine Meyers Brandchaft, was a social worker and her father, Bernie Brandchaft, was a leading psychoanalyst. Brandchaft was himself interested in Klein's work and spent some time in London assimilating her approach. However, he moved on to become a leading follower of Kohut and then developed his own version of interpersonal analysis. Priscilla was the oldest of three girls, all of whom became therapists, and all of whom spent time training in London. She arrived at the age of 25 with her first husband Anthony Roth, a successful art dealer and historian, and later, after his tragic death, married Nicholas Garland the political cartoonist.

Priscilla began training as a child Psychoanalytical at the Tavistock Clinic and then moved on to train at the British Psychoanalytical Society, where she went on to become a training analyst and a sought-after supervisor. Her training analysis was with the unconventional Leslie Sohn, whose work she admired but did not emulate. She was also greatly influenced by Hanna Segal and Betty Joseph, and was a long-standing member of Betty Joseph's seminar, where I first came to know her work. She was a prominent contributor to the seminar, and subsequently joined Michael Feldman, Ron Britton and me to give papers at the annual West Lodge Conference. She was also close to Ignês Sodré, with whom she worked closely on her papers.

The paper which gives its title to this book, 'Mapping the Landscape', is characteristic of her thinking. The pioneers, perhaps, for her, Freud and Klein, made the original discoveries, and it is the next generation that make detailed maps of the terrain they opened up. In this paper she is concerned to describe how unconscious processes influence both patient and analyst without either of them becoming aware of them. I am sure the reader will be amused by the way she illustrates this when she quotes David Foster Wallace's story in which two young fish, swimming along, meet an older fish who says, 'Morning boys, how's the water?' The young fish asks, 'What the hell is water?' (see Chapter 7). We might ask, as so many people do, what the hell is the unconscious? And we have to be grateful to have it pointed out by the older fish, and also to be forced to take account of it when its neglect becomes so evident. The story made me think that the fish flapping about in the fisherman's boat becomes all too aware of the importance of water once he has lost it. However, what Roth is helping us do is to map the effect of unconscious processes on both the patient and the analyst, and to describe how they influence each other in ways they are not usually aware of.

The various chapters in this book show the variety of her interest, but also the continuity of her approach. This is perhaps an example of what she describes as the unconscious thread, which links thoughts and memories together, and makes a coherent map of otherwise disparate ideas. She is the opposite of stuffy, privately and professionally, sympathetic and generous with her time.

Foreword

Tomasz Fortuna

Priscilla Roth's 'Mapping The Landscape: Levels of Transference Interpretation' (Roth 2001) is now considered a classic text on Kleinian psychoanalytic technique. It is the first paper by the author of this book that I got to know and subsequently taught, among several of her other papers, to clinicians in the UK and abroad. 'Mapping The Landscape' has become the first chapter in her book, and it seemed natural that it would make an excellent title for this book, reflecting Roth's inspiring clinical approach. Priscilla Roth thought that too.

This deeply clinical text demonstrates the complexity of the interaction and relational nuance in the process of psychoanalytic work with the transference and countertransference dimensions of the analytic situation. This is also the way I experienced her as her former supervisee, a learning clinician and a younger colleague analyst. Roth is a psychoanalyst who is able to stop and reconsider her position, her point of view, and continuously invite a dialogue with her patients and her students. She supervised and taught candidates and analysts all over the world.

The chapters included in this book have been written at different periods of her long clinical career with an intent to communicate, discuss, share and pass on her clinical acumen, her psychoanalytic approach. This is exactly what makes this collection of chapters so harmonious, authentic and resonant with the clinical work we do as analysts, and what it means to be human in relation to another person.

The fundamental attitude of a sensitive clinician for her patients is Roth's not only concern. She has confidentiality of her patients – an essential feature of psychoanalytic work – at heart. Although Roth has written and presented numerous papers, the chapters in this book were carefully selected, material and identities disguised; some papers were previously published, others become available to the reader for the first time. This, however, means that a body of Roth's work presented in confidential settings had to be left out for these very reasons.

The book is divided into two parts. Part I presents Roth's clinical papers, organized thematically rather than chronologically, and Part II comprises an essay and two lectures. Part I consists of seven chapters, starting with 'Mapping the Landscape' and a chapter on projective identification. These first two chapters set the scene for the rest of this section of the book, as Roth's clinical approach and the concepts of identification, representation and idealization, underpinned by the process of projective identification, are present throughout her writings.

Part II consists of two lectures and an important essay. The lectures offer Roth's fresh take on the presence of the ongoing struggle and negotiation throughout one's life of the emotional dilemmas imposed on us by the Oedipal challenge, and the closely linked question of *becoming oneself* and one's identity, with beautiful references to Vladimir Nabokov's auto-biographical work and Roth's poignant description of her experience of supervising therapeutic work with a little boy.

The essay on Klein's ideas of envy and gratitude is part of the introduction written for the book *Envy and Gratitude Revisited* (2008), edited with Alessandra Lemma. This essay is an important contribution to the current psychoanalytic debate on the contemporary significance of those concepts.

The introduction by Ignês Sodré discusses in detail each of the chapters and the main themes present throughout Roth's work and writings. The Preface by John Steiner brings us closer to Roth as a clinician and a private person, with her unique life story and her development as a psychoanalyst.

I feel honoured to have been able to work alongside Priscilla Roth and Ignês Sodré to bring the idea of this book into fruition. I am delighted that Priscilla Roth's book is now available to the reader.

References

Roth, P. (2001) Mapping The Landscape: Levels of Transference Interpretation. *International Journal of Psychoanalysis* 82: 533–543.

Roth, P. and Lemma, A. (2008) *Envy and Gratitude Revisited*. London: Routledge.

Introduction

Ignês Sodré

This is a brilliant book by a master clinician who combines a passion for psychoanalysis with a sympathetic view of the people she works with. Her clinical understanding is subtle and very much her own, and the close examination of her moment-to-moment work, abundantly illustrated in this book, reveals a capacity for imaginative attention. The reader will feel privileged to accompany this analyst and each of her patients in their unique journeys.

In this Introduction I will first attempt to distil the essence of each chapter, and then discuss some of the central aspects of Roth's work – the questions of idealization, of reparation and of the working through in the sessions, as the patient moves towards a capacity to experience the depressive position; and of the understanding of projective and introjective mechanisms, specially of projective identification, in clinical work. These central themes interconnect, forming the *fil rouge* which permeates her work. I hope to convey a sense of who she is: the combination of her clinical acumen and her awareness of her patients' predicament. She says:

> As Klein's work developed it became more central to her understanding and her use of technique to always keep in mind the *profound distress* his destructiveness causes the patient himself: mostly not consciously, but powerfully taking its toll in inhibitions, incapacitating limitations, feelings of persecution, grievances, confusion, and a sometimes paralysing guilt. It is surely one of Klein's greatest gifts that, following Freud, she showed us that the dilemma of human beings is that we have to suffer terribly for our basic impulses.
>
> (Unpublished lecture notes, 2021)

The question of what and when to interpret is at the core of Roth's clinical work, encompassing, as it does, the centrality of the transference as well as the necessity of 'roaming through the internal and external landscape'. Equally essential is the examination of the countertransference, of the analyst's understanding of what is happening in her own internal landscape. When we take on a patient for analysis, we *choose* to embark on a long and difficult journey, navigating on unchartered waters: through emotional

DOI: 10.4324/9781003588870-1

storms as well as in excessively calm seas. 'Acheronta movebo ...' said Freud (quoting Virgil), dramatically and truthfully. Each analysis is unique, powerfully affecting both patient and analyst.

'Mapping the Landscape' (Chapter 1) and 'The Unconscious Thread and the Here and Now' (Chapter 7), the first and the last chapters in Part I of the book, signal the two major concepts – the two directions of the 'explorations' in her formulations of the mind and of analytic work; what she calls 'roaming the landscape' and the ever present unconscious phantasy. At its deepest level, the 'unconscious thread' may also refer to that which may never become entirely conscious, which can only be inferred after a long process of analysis: what Roth refers to as 'the dominant unconscious phantasy'.

Although neither was written for this purpose, these chapters work as pendants, linked together by theme and depth, and as 'manifestos' of Roth's fundamental beliefs.

Part I: Clinical Papers

Chapter 1: Mapping the Landscape: Levels of Transference Interpretation

The first chapter, a classic paper which gives the book its name, vividly illustrates the qualities that define Roth's work. Here she describes what she considers to be four different levels of interpretation; the analyst works on all these levels, moving subtly between them as she approaches, with the patient, the deepest level: focussing on the here and now of the central dynamic between her patient and herself. The work in the session should explore 'the whole landscape in our mind, a free-floating awareness of our experience of our patient's experiences', when attempting 'to understand – to make a map of – what the patient does with difficult and even unbearable states of mind'.

Roth describes four consecutive sessions in detail, illustrating the necessity and purpose of each level of interpretation; each session is part of a frieze, panel following panel until an integrated, live process is comprehended: 'the real conviction about what was going on between the patient and me only came in the final session of the week'.

Chapter 2: Using Projective Identification

The only chapter which is specifically about projective identification, it includes an extensive discussion of the history of the concept and its development in Kleinian theory and clinical practice. The sessions described contain successive moments of projective identifications with versions of the analyst/mother. The hateful analyst she has to protect herself from is seen as a terrifying depressed mother; this is quickly dealt with by a massive projective identification with a mother who is frightening in her cruelty to a child. An unconscious phantasy as to the content of her analyst's mind leads to a projective identification with a mother whose pregnancy is experienced as a triumphant cruelty to a 'monstrous' child.

Suddenly something unexpected happens: a change in the way of interpreting opens space; saying 'I'm wondering how to say to you what I'm thinking' Roth creates a more benign atmosphere between analyst and patient. The patient is now able to be in contact with her vulnerability, aware of the loss of precious time; the last session ends with moving material about the difference between claustrophobic walls, and a couch with baby-protective bars: she feels held by her analyst. 'At this moment the patient is not in projective identification with one or another malevolent or benign version of her analyst. She is herself, and has more fluid identifications with ... her objects.'

Chapter 3: Being True to a False Object: A View of Identification

Here, in her first published paper, Roth demonstrates her capacity to reach beyond the false, towards the truth of the reparative wish to rescue and protect the good object: to discover the love behind the suspiciousness and contempt.

Roth follows Deutsch's seminal paper on 'As-If' personalities, and Riesenberg-Malcolm's further contribution, with her own original view. 'Shallow falseness' is the result of an identification perceived as false, but dependent on the falseness never being recognised. Her patient unconsciously protects her mother – the analyst in the transference – and herself from catastrophic depression. 'The false object is the closest thing to a good object that is available.' Being able to understand that these identifications in her patient have not only a pathological function but are part of a process of reparation is both illuminating and moving.

Chapter 4: Absolute Zero: A Man Who Doubts His Own Love ...

Roth starts with, 'Fundamental to Kleinian thought is the belief that the early ego coheres around its experiences of a good object. This is the beginning of psychic structure.'

This chapter's central concern is what happens when the good object is felt to be lost, not just temporarily, but as if it had never existed: past experiences with the good object are felt to be a sham. Roth describes moments in an on-going analysis when a violent crisis of mistrust takes over – shockingly and unexpectedly for the analyst: 'The patient feels internally and externally attacked to such an extent that he feels his survival depends on his somehow escaping from what feels like a profoundly threatening experience.'

Powerful manic defences are used to survive the terror of depression and internal catastrophe; this manifests itself in a hidden contemptuous attitude to the analyst; behind this the patient, apparently idealizing of the analyst, is threatened by despair: Freud's 'a man who doubts his own love may, no must, doubt every lesser thing'. 'Idealization is not love with a little bit of extra enthusiasm tagged on. Idealization is the opposite of love.'

Chapter 5: 'I Used to Think You Were Wonderful': The Persecution/ Idealization Cycle of Melancholia

Here Roth explores two versions of Klein's theory of idealization: not contradictory, but importantly different. In version one, the original good object must be experienced as ideal: nothing less would convey 'the whole of (the infant's) instinctual desires': the infant projects his entire loving capacity onto the object, and this projected-into object is then introjected, together with its actual goodness, to become the infant's very core. In version two, idealization comes from a defensive exaggeration of the object's goodness as a safeguard against the fear of the persecuting breast into which hateful feelings and parts of the self have been projected.

Central to the patient's psychopathology is the belief that it is in her object's power to transport her back to when she and her mother/analyst inhabited the paradise lost of perfect mother/perfect baby. The analyst must 'whisk her off' to the ideal breast. She has been there for a moment in the past; the perception of separateness becomes total loss and is accompanied by immense rage and envy. Ordinary life is defined by the experience of longing to be *where she is not*.

Chapter 6: Pity and Disconnection: The Misuse of Metaphor

Roth describes Klein's patient Dick as a prelude to her study of her patient W. The rigidity and impoverishment of this rather strange man is, like in Dick, ultimately connected with his terror of what he imagines he inflicted /can inflict on his objects, and his despair at the impossibility of reparation. On the face of it, W is someone one wouldn't imagine devoting many years to a full analysis. What is revealed through the analytic process is that W suffers from a fear/an almost certainty that he is incapable of love.

Central to the understanding of W's pathology is the idea that the deficit of symbolic thinking comes not from an absence of meaning but from what Klein calls *an uncontrollable proliferation of meanings*. Like Dick, W is too identified with the attacked object. This leads to a premature empathy, and a confusion between persecutory anxiety and primitive depressive anxieties. He feels he caused irreparable damage; and love is too frail to repair it. In the course of the analysis W began 'to tolerate feeling some pity and some gratitude towards his objects'. He has discovered what he calls 'metaphors': an important development, though these are still symbolic equations, rather than symbolic thinking. But moments of real tenderness also begin to be experienced, both in external reality and in the positive transference.

Chapter 7: The Unconscious Thread and the Here and Now

In this chapter Roth draws on a 1958 clinical seminar given by Klein:

> When we keep in mind ... 'the unconscious thread' then we cannot help linking. ... We know that what comes now, which might look entirely different, nevertheless has a connection with what came earlier in the session. Later, at two or three points in the session we remember what was said in the last session, or what happened three months ago. ... Or suddenly we remember a dream that completely clarifies the situation. ... When we can keep [the unconscious thread] in mind ... we find we have helped the patient to bring about a degree of integration and synthesis, which is one of the most important tasks in analysis.

Roth is thinking of an organic process, continuously in the background of the mind, coming to the front at particular moments, illuminating movements in the process; in the patient it is unconscious, in the analyst, pre-conscious:

> It takes a long time to get a convincing picture of a patient's dominant unconscious phantasy: what we do along the way is critical to this endeavour and must, first of all, *ensure that we are not interfering with its emergence into the transference or with our own gradually developing awareness of it. Sometimes we may pay such close attention to what we feel our patients are doing from moment to moment in the session that we fail to pay attention to the underlying story and hence miss an opportunity to identify it.*

At the most fundamental level, primitive phantasies 'influence and eschew our perceptions and experiences' and can 'completely determine the way we see the world' but may never reach consciousness.

The clinical material here comes from when the patient's analysis is coming to an end. The patient describes a trip to 'the only place she'd even felt she belonged to', but where she can't stay. This is a different position from the earlier, compelling belief that the ideal world could become real: thus, she suffers a profound but temporary depression. She has to face 'the reality of reality'. The chapter ends with a horrible dream, a cruel version of separation and separateness, suffered by the Object; but the Object suffers *for her* – a depressive position dream, cruel but dominated by sadness (hers for the analyst, the analyst's for her). Grief and sorrow.

Part II: Lectures and Essay

Chapter 8: The Oedipus Complex Can Never Be Fully Resolved

In this deceptively simple chapter, arguing against the idea that the Oedipus complex could ever be worked through enough to disappear from our minds, Roth uses the clinical example of a few consultations with a couple, both in individual analyses, but nevertheless absolutely stuck, with their child, in a distressing situation that seems unresolvable to all three.

Here Roth describes an Oedipal triangle, where father, mother and their third child, a fourteen year old boy, seemed to be careering towards a domestic catastrophe: a previously well-functioning family of a couple with three children becoming stuck in a tormenting situation leading towards the enactment of an Oedipal tragedy. Roth's brief contact with this couple led to understanding the various projective identification processes: turns of the kaleidoscope produced, for each parent and for their communications to, and about, each other, different configurations playing confusedly and too intensely at the same time, invisibly to the couple, each caught up as well in their own powerfully Oedipal transference to the consultant.

Chapter 9: On Becoming Oneself: Nabokov and The-One-Who-Isn't-Super-Pig

This chapter, which brings together the delightful three-year-old Nabokov of *Speak Memory* and a moving study of a very disturbed, and, to start with, the opposite of delightful seven-year-old boy, and his transformation into the happy, very likeable little boy he could potentially be, is a joy to read, as well as a profound understanding of the transformative psychoanalytic process that leads to the capacity to become oneself. It starts by examining her psychoanalytic and philosophical views in relation to the fundamental question of identity: 'Who am I?'

After little Nabokov's discovery of time, through the experience of who he is when 'strutting' between his mother and his father, Roth brings us Justin: 'Justin felt he could not cope with his awful feelings of smallness, which made him believe himself to be incapable of saving his parents from his attacks on them inside himself.' He imagined that everything had been polluted, and couldn't trust in the continuity of the love of his parents. He had projected into and massively identified with a superior, contemptuous object; this identification had taken over as if it were the self, which had serious consequences for the effective personality. His treatment brought him back to being himself with his own capacities, no longer defined by *who he is not.*

Chapter 10: Melanie Klein on Envy

In this chapter Roth explores the fruitfulness and complexity of Klein's 1957 essay 'Envy and Gratitude', which she describes as 'a culmination of her previous work and a radical addition to it'. This book created an immediate controversy, focussed on Klein's postulating the existence of a constitutional envy, even though she emphasized its interaction, from the beginning, with external conditions.

What defines this chapter, and makes it particularly helpful, is the clarity and depth with which Roth examines the development of the theory and its consequences for clinical understanding. One example: she describes envy interfering with one of the infant's most necessary defences, bi-polar splitting, difficultating the introjection of the good/ideal breast, essential for the organization and strengthening of the early ego.

The second part of the chapter explores different clinical questions: narcissism, separateness and separation; defences; and triangularity. Roth ends with 'What is Gratitude?', saying that according to Klein, the appeasement of hunger brings satiation, but not gratitude; this comes from 'the pleasure and delight from smell and from touch, from gazing and being gazed at, from being held comfortably and safely. It contains all the budding sensory and psychological experiences which will gradually become what we know as love.'

Some Central Themes

Identity, Identification and the Use of Projective Identification

Three chapters refer to identity and identification in their titles: Chapter 2, 'Using Projective Identification'; Chapter 3, 'Being True to a False Object'(subtitled 'A View of Identification'); and Chapter 9, 'On Becoming Oneself'. These concepts appear everywhere in the book; the understanding of projective identification is fundamental to Roth's systematic examination of the countertransference. Chapter 2 starts by summarizing Klein's theory; the clinical material is particularly helpful because it shows the movement, within one session, of rapidly changing identifications: with a cruel, cold mother, then a transformation of the vulnerable self into a 'monstrous child', with an almost unbearable tormenting of the analyst; the session ends with a change in the transference and countertransference in which the patient, finally feeling held by the analyst, becomes more herself. Chapter 3 focuses on an identification with a false object, including an identification with a ridiculous version of the analyst/ mother. This often repeated identification helps the analyst to understand the dynamics of the mother/child relationship in the internal world, and what is being defended against by idealization, seen as primarily needed by the Object. In Chapter 9, a child is in massive projective identification with 'Super-Pig', who has taken over the omnipotent qualities of his objects whilst the self is defined by a negative identity: by not being his vulnerable, and experienced as inferior, self.

Idealization

Idealization is a concept which appears throughout Roth's work. It is the central theme in Chapter 5, 'I Used to Think You Were Wonderful'; the wish to return to the wonderful past reveals a deep melancholia, a yearning for the paradise lost of an exclusive union between mother and baby, which results in unbearable disappointment, and a grievance which constantly contaminates the patient's relationship with her object. The much more hopeful result of many years in analysis appears in Chapter 7. Here grief and sorrow take the place of grievance and melancholia; achieving separateness is painfully experienced, but necessary, and involves the recognition of the object's love for her.

This concept is also central, in strikingly different ways, in two other chapters: In Chapter 3, 'Being True to a False Object', idealization is discovered to be part of a process of reparation of the false, but ultimately fragile and despairing object: a cure for the object's depression, and the patient's own.

In Chapter 4, 'Absolute Zero', we see again a different version: here idealization is used to protect the analyst and the patient from his contempt and rage against her, and ultimately from the terror of destruction and the despair of no love.

Reparation

Reparation, (or the incapacity of making reparation) is an essential concept for Roth, permeating the whole book, and appearing in many different, sometimes surprising, ways in the clinical situations.

After reading Chapter 3, 'Being True to a False Object' one realizes that the title itself implies something reparative: the identification with the false object, central to the severe psychopathology, ultimately has a benign, reparative function: 'being true' also refers to a fundamental loyalty to the damaged object whose goodness has to be retrieved. In Chapter 4, 'Absolute Zero', making reparation is for a long time impossible: what stops it is not hatred for the object, but despair about the melancholic's experience of his incapacity to love. The patient in Chapter 6, 'Pity and Disconnection', who is much more damaged and whose capacity to think symbolically is almost inexistent, lives in terror of depressive anxiety: he is persecuted by the damaged loved object. The patient in Chapter 5 believes, with powerful conviction, that there is a (both hated and loved) omnipotent object who *should*, and *could*, make reparation to her by recreating an original paradise of two: a perfect mother and a perfect baby.

The road towards the depressive position

Central to Roth's Kleinian point of view is the belief that the trajectory towards growth and development implies a gradual movement towards the capacity to experience the depressive position. This is never static: we all move between positions, in a fluid oscillation which implies – necessitates – a going backwards and forwards, at the threshold between paranoid-schizoid and depressive position. Roth's minutely detailed clinical material makes it possible to observe these fluctuations clearly and convincingly: inside of, and between, the sessions, and in the understanding of the psychoanalytic process, in a particular period of an analysis or at its conclusion. Every chapter describes the movement towards, and the stepping back from, this trajectory: what the patient is willing/able to understand further, and what is felt to be unbearable.

Part I
Clinical Papers

1   Mapping the Landscape

Levels of Transference Interpretation

Priscilla Roth

In *A Clinician's Guide to Reading Freud*, Peter Giovacchini gives some material from his practice, which I would like to borrow in order to discuss some interesting issues it raises:

> During analysis, a 27-year-old woman patient of mine dreamed that she was at a dance. The setting was hazy, but she was able to see the grey suit worn by a man who asked her to dance. They danced around the room, and suddenly her partner steered her to a corner and pressed himself against her. She could feel his erect penis. Inasmuch as I often wore grey suits and the transference was clearly erotic, I believed this dream was an obvious allusion to her sexual feelings toward me. I also knew she was struggling with and defending herself against her impulses. Wishing to pursue this theme, I asked her to free-associate to the dream because she was inclined to pursue other seemingly unrelated topics. She hesitantly considered some of the dream elements, such as its haziness. I then direc-ted her attention to the man in the grey suit. She was silent for approxi-mately a minute and then became, what seemed to me, tremendously anxious. She finally reported a sensation of intense dizziness, feeling that the couch was spinning furiously. Gradually these feelings subsided, and she continued talking but made no reference whatsoever to the dream. I became immensely curious and had to interrupt her and ask her about the dream. She naively answered: 'What dream?' To my astonishment, she had forgotten it completely. I then repeated the dream to her and was able to help her remember it. Once again, I brought her attention to the man in the grey suit, and once more she felt the couch spinning and totally wiped the dream from her memory. I tried a third time and with the same results. As she experienced these spinning sensations, she described a vortex that was sucking her thoughts into it. Certainly, the memory of her dream seemed to be pulled into the hidden recesses of her mind.
>
> (Giovacchini, 1982, p. 13)

Giovacchini uses this material to discuss (and reject) the concept of primal repression. I am making use of it now to raise a different issue: the question

DOI: 10.4324/9781003588870-3

of how we choose what we interpret to our patients – what level we come in at or 'go for'. I chose this material because it is clear, vivid and direct, and not too complicated, and because it seems to me it can be understood in several different ways.

In the first place, it is, one suspects, 'about' the patient's father, possibly her actual, external father, but almost certainly her image of a father, her internal father. In this respect the vignette is reminiscent of Freud's Dora case: Herr K and Dora's father, pressing themselves upon her. Giovacchini doesn't, in this session, interpret this. 'Your dream is about your father; you are afraid to know you have these thoughts about your father' is an interpretation that one could imagine Freud, at the time of Dora, making to this patient. And it would probably be, in one sense, true.

'You are afraid of your dream because your dream is about me.' As I understand it, this is the level at which Giovacchini understood his patient's material. What he shows us is an analyst in a session, trying to talk to his patient in the session, about thoughts she had about him in the middle of the night called a dream. 'I often wear grey suits, the man in the dream wore a grey suit – in the middle of the night you had this fantasy about me.' This is an interpretation about the transference of specific qualities, somewhat isolated and discreet – and these are dealt with from a distance.

But there are other ways of looking at this material, of course. Other levels of meaning that in no way negate the meanings I've already mentioned, but add something else as well. For example: one might, as the analyst, feel and say something like, 'There is something going on in this session, now, in which I, interpreting to you, am being perceived as the man in the dream. It is as if the dream is repeating itself here.' In this case the woman in the session and the woman having the dream are one and the same person; as is the analyst. The dream itself might be seen as a picture of the patient's view of her relationship with her analyst; a picture of which she is not fully aware, but which emerges in the session as well as in the dream.

Further, and closely related, we might consider the ways in which some combination of the patient's pressure, and the difficulties this stirs up in the analyst, lead to an unconsidered response by the analyst to create this situation – an internal relationship is in fact being enacted within the session, an enactment in which both analyst and patient are taking part.

When this happens, as it does in every analysis, the most important interpretation the analyst will make is to himself; in the Giovacchini example, he might ask himself, 'Why do I find myself repeatedly pushing the patient into a corner? Why am I pressing my questions on her?' Having dealt with that in his own mind, he is then much freer to consider how to address his patient. He might, for example, in some situations, say something like, 'We seem to have arrived at a situation in which I am repeatedly pursuing you, or pushing you into a corner in a way that frightens you, like in your dream.'

For the purposes of this paper, I don't want to go into how such an impasse comes about, or whose fault it is. It is essential for every analyst to think about who is pulling whom into the action, but what I want to focus on here is the different levels that are operating simultaneously – because as analysts we have to choose the most useful place to intervene.

There are certainly moments in every analysis where one would say, 'This is your father you are afraid of, and you feel that the man in the grey suit is your father' (a 'level 1' interpretation). There are also times when there is a view of the analyst in a dream that is not at all ego-syntonic to the patient: it happens in the middle of the night, as it were, and the patient in the session has no knowledge or recognition of it. So that as the analyst in the session you are trying to introduce your patient to aspects of herself and her internal object relationships that she doesn't consciously experience or know about (level 2). And much of the day-to-day work in analysis also concerns the way in which patients feel we are enacting, and indeed pull us to enact in the session the scenarios of their inner world – in order to maintain an internal status quo, to reassure themselves about their view of the world, and so on (level 3). In fact, this enactment may sometimes, unfortunately, be necessary for us to be aware of what is going on, and as analysts we must be alert to the part played in this by our own anxieties and defence mechanisms (level 4). So, we have to have this whole landscape in our mind, with all these levels of interaction, levels of internal and external reality. We have to be able to allow a kind of free-floating awareness of the different levels of our experience of our patients' experiences. Then we have to decide where it is most useful to intervene. But we must always remember that in choosing to focus our attention on one aspect of the patient's communication we must, in our minds, hold on to and be aware of the other aspects as well.

Clinical Material

At this point I will present some more extensive clinical material of my own, so that we can look at this process in more detail.

My patient is a 35-year-old South American woman. She is tall and slim, and an outstanding feature is her great mass of curly red hair. As a small child she lived alone with her mother for several years while her father travelled on business. Her mother is described as gay, beautiful and Bohemian; her father, who lived with them more permanently from the time my patient was about 3 years old, was a steady older man who was referred to by the patient and her mother as 'our rock'.

The patient is now married with three children – a daughter, A; a little boy, B; and a baby girl, C, now 8 months old. She has her own small market research company and at the time I am reporting had been engaged in a new project that presented her with what looked like good opportunities for her future. Because this project was underfinanced and speculative, she was employing students and part-time temporary workers. Her husband was a successful businessman, but the financial circumstances of the family fluctuated wildly. This presented problems about paying my fees, and several months had passed without her paying me. She had good excuses, but at the same time, she seemed not to be taking the problem seriously. I found myself very uncertain about what to do: I knew this woman could be very disturbed and disturbing, and that she badly needed her analysis; experience had made me feel that her children were in some danger if her analysis ended. So, I therefore let the situation continue for too long. Consciously I was worried about her state of mind and about her children. In retrospect, there must have been unconscious reasons, too, why I waited too long to be firm with her: wanting to be liked by my patient, being too content to be idealized and insufficiently suspicious of her seductiveness and so on. But she began to get into a manic state, and became more and more dictatorial, with me and at home, and I began to realize that my lack of firmness about the money was contributing to that. I was also increasingly aware of my resentment of her treatment of me. So, I addressed what I thought was going on and became much firmer with her, referring to the dangerous effects on her of what she was doing to me by not paying me, and conveyed to her that it had to be taken seriously.

I want to present the Wednesday and Thursday sessions of a week shortly after this, but I will first give a brief summary of the Monday and Tuesday sessions as background.

Monday

She told me that she had spent the weekend working on the project – she had a difficult meeting with her staff who complained she didn't let them do their jobs: she redid the questionnaires, changed all the arrangements – in her words, 'rewrote the script', in major ways. She had invited everyone to her country cottage for the weekend; she now thought this was a mistake as it had obviously made them envious, since they are mostly unemployed and she has a lovely house: her maid kept walking through, the children's nanny was there and the gardener. She said how difficult it must have been for these struggling people to have to observe all this.

The patient's tone of voice and manner of speaking was striking and conveyed a very particular attitude; she was speaking, as the French say, *de haut en bas*. I thought she was taking me on a kind of tour of her lovely, rich, full life and that I was meant to be full of admiration and envy.

Briefly, I suggested to her that as she was describing her weekend, I thought she felt me to be like the 'struggling staff', enviously watching her with all she had. I said I thought her need for this kind of situation between us had been particularly provoked by her realization that she needed her analysis and therefore was going to have to pay me, and that her description of the weekend seemed to be her attempt to reverse what she might otherwise feel at the weekend: how determined she was that she be the enviable centre of everything, and how awful it would be for her to have to know about my centrality for her.

Tuesday

She referred back to Monday's session and the interpretation I had made to her, and said that in fact there was something she hadn't said about the weekend; not just this weekend, but what happened at weekends: she went mad. This weekend she shouted and screamed at her husband for not being available to her, for always being at work, keeping her at a distance and being cut off from her. She had screamed at him and she had hit him. The children were in the room – it often happened this way, she said, that the children were there while she and her husband had these violent fights. She had then decided that she simply 'had to' tell her oldest daughter how suspicious she was about her husband's business trips to Europe – she was 'sure' he was having an affair, and thought the daughter ought to know. The implication was that the daughter's father was doing something filthy, sexual and corrupt, and the daughter ought to know this.

I told her I thought she wanted me to know how she couldn't contain and hold inside herself her rage with me over the weekend – the real weekend experience as opposed to the reversed weekend experience she had told me about on Monday. I linked her attacks on her husband to this rage with me, for not being available. She was silent. I felt she was listening. I then said something more: I said that I thought her furious fights with her husband had to be observed by her children because they have to be the observers of the passion and violence of the sexual parents – a view of them originating in her own violent attacks on them.

I said that while she insisted that she felt nothing about my weekends – no disturbance, no curiosity – nor about my relationship with the man who answered the telephone when she phoned at my home – she showed us that there was a child who was to be horrified and appalled and furious at what a parent was doing – but that it was not going to be her, it would be her children, especially her daughter. I said she made her daughter have these feelings, which she felt were unbearable for her to have herself.

Comment

Within the Monday session there is a description of the weekend, which I could interpret along the lines of 'when you say them you mean me'. I am 'them' (the poor, eager-to-be-employed workers) who are made envious by all her possessions. I thought she was projecting envy into the employees, standing for me. At the same time, she treated me with contempt more directly by not paying me, and I thought that all this behaviour served as a defence against her own envy, or a defence against acknowledging my importance as her analyst. She makes herself the centre of everything. In terms of Giovacchini's example, this is along the lines of: the man in the grey suit is me. The poor, envious employees on the weekend were me (level 2).

By the time I made this interpretation on Monday, I had worked through and overcome my sense of impotence about her not paying me; I was not angry with the patient, nor did I feel contemptible. I felt strong enough and confident enough about my positive feelings towards the patient to interpret to her in a way that was firm, but wouldn't put her down.

Interpreting in this way on the Monday enabled her to bring the really bad acting out – the real weekend experience – on the Tuesday. My interpretation of the Tuesday material (highly summarized) took as its focus what was going on 'out there' – at the weekend, with her family, but as an introduction to what was going on in here, in order to be able to elucidate her inner world:

> You have a kind of dream going on inside you in which I am engaged in being part of a couple, which makes you feel horribly jealous and which you violently attack in your jealous rage. Attacked, this couple becomes violent in nature and you act this out with your husband and make your children bear the distress of it.

This is a strong interpretation, and when making it I am counting on several things about her, but most importantly, what I know of her capacity to bear some guilt.

I had to wait until the following session to see how the patient dealt with this interpretation. I will have more to say about these interactions, and how I understand them, at a later point in this paper. The following two sessions I will look at in detail.

Wednesday

She told me that she had been in a terrible panic, the night before she couldn't sleep because of it. She was absolutely panicking about pollution. (This was in July, and it was very hot.) She spoke for a long time – the radio reported how very high the pollution level was and she was terrified about it and what it would do to them all. She felt there was poison all around. She had closed all the windows, but you couldn't get away from it. She was clearly very anxious.

I thought that she was telling me what she had done with what I had said to her in the previous day's session. This had centred on her telling me about putting very painful, horrible feelings into her children, and today's session was about millions and millions of infinitesimally small particles that were poisoning her children, her husband and herself. I had to make the decision in my own mind whether she felt I had been poisoning her on the previous day, by saying things about her that were felt to be cruel and murderous, or whether she was primarily talking about what she had done with the threat of guilt from the previous day's session. My feeling was that it was the latter. I thought this was her way of dealing with the guilt she was threatened with experiencing when she began to see what she was doing to her children, and behind that, to me in her mind. She had projected the poison into the atmosphere, and it therefore was not experienced as coming from her, but as coming from the outside; the guilt not experienced inside her mind causing her pain, but broken and fragmented into bits and then coming back at her from outside. I am aware that the brevity of my description of the Monday and Tuesday sessions may make it difficult for some readers to be convinced that the Wednesday material was in response to Tuesday's session. I was convinced both by the seriousness of the patient's response on the Tuesday and by the level of anxiety on the Wednesday that the 'pollution' she was afraid of on Wednesday was linked to the session on the Tuesday.

I felt that what she needed me to do was to bring these confusing bits of her experience together, to show her how painful these feelings were, but to assume she could, with my help, know about and bear them.

I therefore reminded her about yesterday's session when she had told me about the very poisonous feelings that she had pushed into all her children, and particularly her oldest daughter. I said she was afraid to know what she felt about me at the weekend, and about her parents in her mind, so she projected these feelings into her children. Then, because she also loved her children and didn't want to hurt them, she was in danger of feeling very guilty about this. Such guilt was too painful for her; therefore she had expelled it, and the poison, the awful badness, was in the air around them all – not in her.

There was a sharp intake of breath, and then, after a moment, she said, 'It is awful. You know, if there was a fire, I'd lay my life on the line for my children. But I can do this.' She paused. Then: 'Isn't it terrible what we can do to those we love?'

I said how frightening it was to be aware of what she did to her children. And then, after a moment, I said I thought she in fact couldn't bear to think about it, and so she had to change it, disperse it around the world to 'what we do to those we love' – to make it not so much her, and her children, but general, all over the place. She was thoughtful for a moment and then said, 'You mean I don't really take it on.'

At this moment in the session I am keeping her attention on what I think she needs to know about, and I am still directing myself to what happens between her and her children. I am not addressing what is happening here, between her and me. I am acutely aware that the epicentre of the difficulties she is talking about is in her relationship with me in the transference. The jealousy, the sense of abandonment, her anger, have their source originally, of course, in her earliest object relations and now in her ongoing phantasies about her and me. But the location of all these feelings has shifted, defensively, to what is going on with her family, and I do address what is going on in her family and how it seems to be affected by what has been going on inside her and between us.

In this sense I am still located in a level 2 area of interpretation. I am interpreting in the transference, but in the transference as it manifests itself outside the immediate here and now of the session. I want to emphasize that I am talking about complex transference manifestations: the way in which the patient uses projective identification to rid herself of unbearable feelings and to maintain her sense of equilibrium, the effects such projective man-oeuvres have on her, and so on.

But I am very aware that all the time she and I are there in the room talk-ing about these things I have not suddenly become neutral to her. The transference relationship (what I referred to earlier as level 3) is going on all the time, and I am aware of it, and wait for the moment when I can address it with her. At this point in the session, we still had about twenty minutes left, and I was reasonably comfortable about allowing the session to develop and the here-and-now relationship between us to become clearer.

After a few minutes she said she had been thinking about her father. He used to be quite nice to her, probably to please her mother, who adores her. (Her actual words were, 'to keep mama sweet'.) But once when she was very little and her mother was out, she had fallen down and cut her forehead. And she had screamed and screamed. And her father had sat her on the kitchen table and washed off the cut and put a plaster on it and said to her, 'Now just stop all that wailing. Your mother's not here now.' She had thought that was tough and hard of him … calling her bluff.

I said I wondered if perhaps she felt me now to be like the father in the story. That when I insisted that she had to pay me, and when I made her face what she was doing to me and to her family, she felt that a nice, soft, mal-leable me – like her mother who adored her – had gone away, and that she was left with a tougher, harder father – me, who she doesn't feel will be seduced by her cries. I said I think she thinks there is a seducible me – like her mother – who lets her get away with things, lets her get away with not paying me, for instance, and a tougher harder me who won't be seduced, and she's afraid she is now stuck alone with this father aspect of me.

I was now addressing a picture of what was going on between us. The underlying transference relationship seemed to me to be level 3. She was quiet for a minute and started to speak about her baby girl:

> She won't be put down; you go to her, you leave her to cry for forty minutes, she won't stop, she just goes on and on and tries to burrow into your neck – she won't be put down. But she's so vulnerable, she's, just a baby – so I can't leave her, I can't put her down.

I said I thought this was a picture of a monster baby, not, I thought, a picture of C, except as she feels it at that moment, but a picture of herself who uses her vulnerability for absolute power.

She said, 'What do you mean?'

I said I thought that it was very painful and hard for her to begin to be aware that she thought I was sometimes forced, by my fears for her very real vulnerability, to pay for her life (her analysis, her servants, etc.). When she didn't pay me, I was, in fact, paying for her to live as she liked – and she felt I was unable to put her down. She said, 'Yes'. It was the end of the session.

Comment

In retrospect, I think I did not properly address in this session what had happened when the patient went from 'I can do this to my children' to 'Isn't it terrible what we can do to those we love?' While being aware of the denuding of meaning in this material, and of the use the patient made of her vulnerability outside the analysis, and how that affected my behaviour, I missed something very important about what was going on within the session: that her understanding of the interpretation ('I can do this to my children') quickly became an appeasement of me, a seduction of me – it's what she uses to keep me 'sweet'. To go from 'I' (what 'I do') back to 'we' (what 'we do'). In fact, I wasn't seduced – I showed her that she didn't take the interpretation in. But what I didn't see at that point was the degree to which her seductiveness pervaded the whole analysis. I think my not falling for it brought the father material – she now felt she had, for the moment at least, been abandoned by her adoring mother, and was with a firm, hard father. Following that, she reminded me about the monster baby who would not be put down: who I think felt quite sure at that point about getting the adoring mother back again.

So, I did not act out with the patient; I was not seduced, but I hadn't really understood the subtleties and pervasiveness of the seduction that was going on. Like Giovacchini interpreting his patient's dream, I was ignoring the way we were playing things out within the session.

Thursday

She was several minutes late, was silent and then said she was so sleepy, so tired. 'I just can't engage', she said.

I said it was the end of the week, her last session for the week, and that earlier in the week she had warned us about what happened at weekends, 'The real madness is at weekends', she had said on Tuesday. But now she was disengaged.

Here I think I was trying to put her in touch with feelings she had been engaged with earlier in the week and to show her what she might be disengaged from.

'Mmmm.' Long silence.

> When you said yesterday, about my panic ... when you explained it in terms of ... you know, the pollution, when you talked in terms of an expression of resistance, to do with something else, the analysis ... well, I was thinking ... I often get a panicky feeling in aeroplanes, too. I can't bear flying.

Then quite a long story about having to take a boat to the Continent last year because she hated going on aeroplanes. 'I wondered about it ... in relation to my preoccupation with the pollution.' There was a pause. Then she started again:

> Your explanation about my panic had a kind of simple meaning ... I've wondered why everyone isn't panicking about the pollution ... and I thought, 'I am afraid to fly ... she is right ... I do organize my life, organize everything not to have to think.'

I felt very uneasy about this material. I didn't doubt that it was factually true – I knew, in fact, that she was afraid to travel by aeroplane.

But I thought it was emotionally not what it was appearing to be – I thought she was still disengaged, but trying to seduce me by saying what she thought I would want to hear. So, I said I thought there was something going on under the surface of her words now – that she seemed to me to be saying something like, 'Why not have a conversation about my problems with air travel ... we could extend yesterday's discussion to a related problem' ... but that I thought that this was an invitation to a dishonest situation – a kind of make-believe analysis.

I think here I was aware of a quality in the session that I had missed on the previous day: the way the patient tried to, and sometimes actually could, seduce me into believing we were working, when, in fact, what was going on was something else – a seductive, mutual-admiration society. On the previous day, I had seen how she had denuded the agreement ('I can do this to my children') of meaning. What I hadn't seen was how it was an attempt to appease and seduce me. With this Thursday session, the seduction had become clearer ... or, at least, clearer to me. So that now the interpretation I made to her is a level 3 and indeed level 4 interpretation as well, because it is taking into account my recognition of my own strong feelings about what is going on between us. It is not addressing her words but it is addressing the woman who is presenting the words, and my feeling about the pressures in this session.

She grumbled for a moment: 'I'm tired, it's Thursday'. And then, after a minute or two, she suddenly said:

> I had a dream last night. Yesterday I had gone to see Stephen to ask if we could use his sound studio to record in. In the dream I went to see Stephen and he asked me to be his assistant, give him some help on the project I am actually in charge of. I thought to myself, 'I have moved beyond that'. In the dream I went to the toilet ...

At this point in the telling of the dream she broke off to add an association:

> Here in this building the first-floor toilet is broken. There is a sign on the door telling you to use the ones on the other floors. But in fact it is not

the toilet itself that is broken – only the handle of the door – the only problem is that the door doesn't lock. Somebody was in the other toilet yesterday morning and so I went to the one with the sign, the one saying, 'Don't use'. But only the door handle is broken so I took a chance and put my bag by the door.'

Here the association ended and she went back to the dream:

> In the dream I was in the loo. In a building. In a school or something. Stephen asked me to participate – I thought, 'I am doing this because I am helping out, assisting him. I'm not sure I want to be involved and anyway I really have moved on from this.' I was feeling very good – the kind of really good feeling I have about my project. Then there was a purple flex, like a light fixture, it was very unusual: very pretty and glittery and purple. I spun it round and twirled it; it was pretty. And then it began to unravel – with those horrid black wires you get inside … I saw they could split and were live, and I thought they must be dangerous.

She paused. 'I was feeling very good in the dream. And I thought, 'I've moved on'. I think that is what the dream was about.'

I said I thought her dream was about the dangerous state of mind she is in. I said I think she feels I am like Stephen in her dream: asking her to participate in her analysis – while she feels so good and feels she has 'moved on' from being my patient who needs analysis to being the director, the producer and organizer. She will help me out, by paying me, and also, as I think she was doing earlier in the session, by seeming to pick up my interpretation, seeming to participate in her analysis – but it is a performance and she actually feels quite superior about it. I linked this to the toilet: the rules aren't for her. The no entry signs aren't for her. She tells herself it is because her need is so great – but I think it is her desperate need to feel that she can break all the rules, break all the boundaries. Which I think makes her think she actually unravels me.

She said, 'Oh'. And then, 'Yes'.

After a moment I pointed out the purple dress I was wearing.

She said, 'Were you wearing that dress yesterday?' When I answered yes, she said, 'Well, the flex was just that colour purple.'

I'll just point out here that we have come full circle back to Giovacchini's material: the man in the grey suit is me – the purple flex is me. I said I think when she feels she will help me out by paying me, by participating because I want her to, like earlier in the session, she feels she is making me in my purple dress twirl and dance about; that she can fiddle with me, saying 'isn't it pretty', seducing me to be pretty, to 'keep me sweet'. But that I thought some part of her, at least in the dream, seems to know there is something black and dark and ugly and dangerous around.

She was silent for a few minutes. Then she said:

> It is a relief. When I feel I am a special case ... I always feel I am a special case, somehow ... but that is never a relief. But when you say what you say ... I suppose it must be being in touch ... it is somehow a relief.

I felt there was a clear difference between this response and what she had been like at the beginning of the session, when I had felt she was trying to seduce me. Here I believed her. It was the end of the session.

In the example from Giovacchini there is a dream, and there is what is going on in the session, and they appear to be two quite separate events. Here we can see the way in which the interaction within the transference, in the analysis, appears in the dream: in both the dream and the analytic sessions she can be full of 'good' feeling, but it is omnipotent feeling – it involves repeatedly engaging in projective manoeuvres in which somebody else (the workers on Monday, her children on Tuesday, the demanding baby on Wednesday, Stephen in the dream; and underlying it all, me in the analysis whenever she feels I can be seduced or managed or handled) has to feel the feelings she can't bear: jealousy, dependency, envy, being needy and therefore, she thinks, contemptible. In this sense the dream is a reflection of the relationship, and the relationship is a reflection of the dream. I believe she could tell me about the dream because sometimes she wants a real understanding, a real knowledge of herself, a real relationship with me, more than she wants to 'feel good', to be a 'special case'. In order to have the sense of really being known, by me and herself, she has to look at the black wires inside the prettiness – the danger inside the feel-good factor. Of course she only can look at this very briefly, and then she has to 'move on'.

Discussion

In his 1972 paper, 'A Critical Appreciation of James Strachey's Paper on the Nature of the Therapeutic Action of Psychoanalysis', Herbert Rosenfeld discusses some aspects of Hannah Segal's 1961 paper given to the Edinburgh Congress:

> She particularly stresses the importance of the analysis of processes of splitting and projection and omnipotence. She gives examples of analytic material where mutative transference interpretations were given. She discusses a patient who complained of disturbances in his capacity to get on with his work. He had projected his greedy destructive dirty part into the analyst and then had denied and dispersed it into many objects in the outside world by whom he felt persecuted. Through a dream where the patient felt invaded and persecuted by smokers, she was able to make a transference interpretation of the analyst as a persecutor who represented, through projective identification, the greedy destructive

parts of the patient. Segal reports that through this analytic experience and similar situations the patient was able to make more contact with the aggressive parts of his self, which strengthened his ego. He also was more able to form a more real relationship to the analyst, which the split off persecutory object relationship had prevented. Segal's description illustrates how transference interpretations can set the mutative process in motion but that this has to be followed up by working-through periods, so that the mutative development can continue and be strengthened. It is important here to be clear that both the detailed transference interpretation and the working through process includes not only the elaboration of the patient's fantasies and behaviour in the transference, but links the patient's conflicts in detail with his present life situation and his past.

                                                        (Rosenfeld, 1972, pp. 456–457)

In the sessions I presented, the real conviction about what was going on between the patient and me only came in the final session of the week, when the material in a dream, and our understanding of its enactment in the transference, came together. At this point the patient and I could fully focus on exploring the vicissitudes of the transference relationship, and the interaction has important meaning for both of us. But to get to this point we have had to roam freely over the landscape of the patient's material. One way this could be described would be to say that for a while I find I am largely making what I have called level 2 interpretations, interpretations that aren't primarily focused on at this moment, in this room. But these, too, are complex, and are attempts to understand – to make a map of – what the patient does with difficult and even unbearable states of mind. When in the Tuesday session I spoke to her about what she had done to her children over the weekend, linking it with her own feelings of outrage about the weekend break from me, I was talking to her about a complicated series of splitting, projections and projective identifications, and then about the effects these projections and projective identifications had on her: how persecuted they made her, or how guilty. Some readers might feel that it would be better to have focused entirely on the projections into the children, and not to have linked these to what was going on in the transference. In fact, I felt convinced that sympathetically understanding her own feelings at being left out, and the jealousy and anger these feelings provoked within her, enabled her to understand why she felt compelled to project such feelings into her children; helped her, that is, to understand what otherwise might have seemed like her arbitrary cruelty. (Of course, I couldn't help but hope that in the end this would enable her not to have to project so massively into her children.)

My point is that in order to get her to moments when she could stop 'moving on' and look at what was inside, I had to be willing to follow her over quite a broad landscape of her experience. I had to be prepared to allow the different levels of her experience to make an impact on me, in order for me to map out the way her internal objects became projected into her family, her colleagues and, very powerfully, into me. In the end I had no doubt that it was in the elucidation of the ongoing transference relationship in the analysis that I could have any real impact on her. But I thought I could not know about this fully, with the sort of richness that reflected the patient's experience, without allowing myself and the patient to roam a bit over the wide territory of her life. So, I did not, could not, interpret only at level 3 and level 4, although I tried continually to make myself aware of, and come back to, what I thought was going on at these levels. My real conviction about the patient's internal world and relationship with her objects only really came about through experiences that enabled me to think and interpret at levels 3 and 4. But I could get to these experiences only by allowing the patient and myself to engage with a wide variety of her experiences.

When we are working well as analysts, we and our patients exist in a very particular emotional landscape. We are continually being used to communicate, enact and reveal the patient's internal dramas. These dramas are in some ways quite simple; their purpose is to maintain the patient's equilibrium, to protect him from overwhelming anxiety, to restore his sense of being able to manage internal and external reality. But the manifold ways in which each patient – and each patient–analyst couple – play out the externalization of these dramas are what define the richness and variety, the very liveliness, of each individual analysis. Our sense of conviction about our patient's internal world comes ultimately from our understanding of the here-and-now transference relationship between us – this is, as I have said, the epicentre of the emotional meaning of an analysis. As analysts we keep one part of our mind located at this level all the time – it is where we somehow always live within the session. This is what I have called levels 3 and 4 of understanding and of interpretation. But I think that much of the filling in, the enrichment, the colour of analysis takes place at a different level, while we become familiar with the quality and variety of our particular patient's particular world.

References

Giovacchini, P. (1982) *A Clinician's Guide to Reading Freud*. New York: Aronson.
Rosenfeld, H. (1972) A Critical Appreciation of James Strachey's Paper on the Nature of the Therapeutic Action of Psychoanalysis. *International Journal of Psycho-analysis* 53: 455–461.

2 Using Projective Identification

Priscilla Roth

In 1946, Melanie Klein described a process by which 'split off parts of the ego are ... projected ... into the mother. This leads to a particular form of identification which establishes the prototype of an aggressive object-relation.' She suggested for these processes the term 'projective identification' (Klein, 1946).

The classic form of projective identification, then, involves putting parts of oneself into an object, so that the object becomes identified with these unwanted aspects of the self. Projective identification is of course an unconscious phantasy – usually a powerful one – in which some quality or attribute or emotional state, belonging to the self, is split off and moved into the object, so that the conscious experience of the subject is that this quality or feeling actually belongs *not to him but* to the other – the object. The picture of the object now contains this quality of the subject. Now, a person may do this for one or more of a number of reasons: he may find this aspect of himself intolerable because it is hateful to him – it would fill him with shame or guilt to have to know that such impulses are actually part of him. Or, importantly, he may do it to control the other person – to manipulate, by forcing disturbing feelings into the other, thus altering his state of mind.

But there is another form of projective identification, and it is a more introjective form: it occurs when someone *takes on* and *takes over* the qualities of someone else, as if they were his or her own. It is a form of identification in which the object's qualities are experienced as one's own, one's possession or one's own qualities and it is almost always accompanied by a projection of some of the subject's own real qualities. I hope to show how this works in the clinical material I will present, but once you are aware of these processes you realize that we can see it all around us in ordinary life: someone is 'being' someone else – 'being' the perfect mother, or 'being' some particularly admired, and envied, professor; a little girl, for instance, 'being' a bossy teacher. What we are 'being' when we take on the characteristics of our objects is a caricature of the object, sometimes subtle, sometimes not so subtle, and we do it for all sorts of reasons: to protect us from anxiety (it is *obviously* easier to cope if one is a teacher than if one is a

DOI: 10.4324/9781003588870-4

little girl), to protect us from envy (I *am* the perfect mother, so I don't need to envy my own mother), to give us a self when we are unsure of who our real self might be.

And while we are 'being' mother or teacher or a particularly wise man, we are projecting our sense of little-ness, of anxiety and uncertainty, into someone else. We all do this. Most of us do it only some of the time and briefly, and we quickly find our own feet and stand in our own shoes again. To do this, we have to take back the feelings we've projected (take back the sense of vulnerability, the knowledge of imperfection and anxiety and envy) and give up the qualities that aren't really ours. And, *when we are well*, most of us manage to do this reasonably well.

There is another point I want to stress about projective identification: when it is used massively and much of the time, it is because it appears to be the best possible solution to what are experienced as uncontainable psychological pressures. The alternative to such states is overwhelming anxiety, genuinely threatening a mental breakdown. It is to avoid psychological catastrophe that people resort to massive use of projective identification, in order to maintain some mental equilibrium.

But there is a price to be paid for such massive shifts of bits of the personality – for moving around the molecules of reality. In the first place, projective identification seriously diminishes the personality – it deprives the subject of his real qualities and capabilities and leaves him intellectually and emotionally thinner. When someone evacuates qualities like greed or rage or fear he also evacuates the part of his mind that is aware of such feelings, and his capacity to think and to know about himself and others is thereby reduced.

And secondly, projective identification is a process, not an event – and it has consequences, which lead to further consequences. When we project anger into another person, we then (by definition) expect that person to be angry with us, and we behave towards him as if he is an angry, threatening persecutor. The person is felt to be threatening both because he contains our anger, and because he is felt to want to get rid of it back into us. It is very much as if there is a quantity of bad unwanted stuff, bad feeling, which will be located either in the subject or in the object, each trying to get rid of it into the other, neither being able to bear having it. Caught up in this vicious circle, the subject may feel the need to attack his object further, or to withdraw in order to protect himself.

The overarching quality, though, of projective identification, is that it communicates states of mind. This is very important, because whether it is *primarily* in order to communicate or is *primarily* designed to evacuate bad feelings, projective identification always happens between people, *in this sense it could be said to be* always object related. Properly understood, it always does communicate something important about the state of mind, the pressures and solutions, the internal objects and the anxieties which the individual uses it to deal with.

In analysis, the most intransigent and frequent use of projective identification is a chronic, not an acute, situation. What we see most often is a state of affairs in which the patient's use of a form of projective identification – of massively introjecting and identifying with an object, and at the same time massively projecting parts of his own personality – has become his mode of being; his very personality could be characterized as not being his own. The problem such a situation presents to us here is that because such a structure is so well established, the analysis of it can be difficult to describe, since of course change takes place so slowly, working through and disentangling the strands of the projections happens over years, not months, certainly not days. So although I will describe several sessions from the analysis of one patient, sessions which I believe demonstrate the presence of processes of projective identification going on within the analysis and manifested within the transference and counter transference, sessions during which these disturbing processes could gradually be studied and understood, sessions, moreover, which I think demonstrate one way of working through such processes – it should be understood that the work in these sessions follows several years of work in which the patient and I have addressed these issues, so that they are more familiar to us both, and we have come to trust in the benefit of our working together.

B is a 40-year-old married woman with two young children. She began five times a week analysis with me a number of years ago. As is true with every patient, B's history is present in every session. Her mother was born in a country torn apart by a brutal war; when mother was 9 years old, her parents sent her to relatives in London to get away from the danger. The story she tells her daughter, my patient, is that from the moment she – mother – arrived in England she became a very good, very happy English girl. Beautiful and highly intelligent, she embraced her new life, living with an English family in the English countryside. But she never wrote to her own parents, nor did she think much about them – she was so relieved to be out of danger that she 'put it all behind her' and started a new life. She never saw them again. She – my patient's mother – did very well at school and eventually gained a high academic degree. Later she met the patient's father and married him. They had two children: my patient and a younger brother. There was a lot of resolute happiness in the family: lots of Christmas celebrations, lots of birthday surprises. The marriage between the parents seems to be a good one, but the reverberations of the mother's monumental tragedy continue, as they must, into the next generation, and the next.

The patient's brother was born when my patient was 2½ years old. B reports this as having been catastrophic. She hated the fact of her brother and she hated her brother. Early in the analysis she talked about the brother's birth as if it had happened that day – 'How would *you* feel?', she asked, as though her brother's birth remained an unforgivable insult.

Shortly after my patient began her analysis, her brother developed a serious illness and died during the third year of the analysis.

The patient remembers herself being very difficult as a child, and she was not liked at school. At 14, at a time when her mother was out of the country working for some months, the patient had her first boyfriend, with whom she had a passionate love affair. She brought the boyfriend home and flaunted him at her father, apparently not caring what father thought, sleeping with him in her bedroom. She made life so difficult for her father that eventually he could no longer tolerate her behaviour and said she had to go to boarding school; he said to mother, 'It's either her or me.'

It is worth saying here that during the first few years of this patient's analysis, there were many times when, in her company, I felt I could see her father's point. She was able to make me feel more terrible, more frustrated and angry and useless, than any patient I ever had. There was a year – the year that her brother was dying – when she sat each day in the chair facing me and subjected me to a cruelty I often thought I could not bear. She is the only patient I have ever had who made me feel physically ill.

She started analysis convinced that her marriage was over. Her relationship with her husband, Charles, was angry and bitter. She was disturbed by the fact that she was having a (first) affair, with S, who she claimed to love passionately but described mostly as an exciting forbidden sexual partner. Her descriptions were full of romantic hyperbole. As the analysis became established, this affair became less urgent and it ended within the first year of analysis; her marriage has become progressively, if unsteadily, more satisfying to both partners.

During these first years of analysis she often felt the whole process to be intolerably frustrating. She had a powerful idealization of what she called 'passionate intensity'; she felt that she needed to be adored and that she would die if she was not. She often said 'I cannot live unless someone is enchanted by me.'

At some point in the first year she told me about an occasion towards the beginning of her affair with S. Her second child was at the time 8 months old and was still being breast fed. The patient wanted her breasts to be full and beautiful, not flat 'like empty envelopes', so she put the baby to bed without feeding her, in order for her breasts to be full for S. I found this story very telling. I thought the incident spoke powerfully about her fear of flat, empty breasts in her object; that is, in the person she needs to care for her – I thought it was probably the mother's depression she feared – and her terror of becoming identified with such a figure. 'Enchanting' is obviously the very reverse of this.

Similarly, a feeling that a session had been 'good' was inevitably followed by a feeling of depression and the thought 'She won't be able to do that again tomorrow'. It became clear that as soon as she gets something that she experiences as good, she is filled with anxiety that it will be all gone; that there will be no more. Empty envelopes.

I came to feel that she lived permanently on a knife edge – never able to count for a moment on the mental robustness or mental whereabouts of her objects. As I came to get her from the waiting room each day, she would look at me with a kind of cold hatred. For a while it actually frightened me, and I found it quite persecuting. But I gradually began to understand that she dealt with a constant anxiety about the state of her objects by a powerful use of projective identification. That is, I came to feel that she was always anxious about whether her object could bear her – bear her powerful feelings and her confusion, bear to think about and know her. And she dealt with this anxiety by herself becoming the cold and hateful figure, and by projecting all the feelings of anxiety into the other.

This situation improved a great deal over the following couple of years, and B became more able to tolerate confusion and anxiety, and to think and work with me about them. But sometimes, in times of particular stress, something disturbing and disorienting – but by now more familiar – started to happen again in the analysis.

The material I am going to present took place during the last two weeks before the summer break beginning at the end of one July. It will, I hope, highlight the way processes of projective identification can come into effect at times of particular stress and anxiety.

In late June, I had had to go away very suddenly for two weeks; the message she was given was that I had to go to the United States because a parent was ill and that I would be in touch with her as soon as I knew when I could be back. On my return – two weeks later and three weeks before the summer break – she was icily angry about everything: resentful that I had come back and staunchly maintaining I ought to have stayed away until September. She was furious that she was going to have to pay attention to me for three weeks. Why should *her* analysis have to be interfered with by *my* life events? 'If your mother' – which she had decided it was – 'has died, you'll be grieving for the next three weeks; if she didn't die, given that she has to be at least 95 years old, you'll be pre-occupied with when it will happen again. Either way, you won't be interested in hearing about me … about my life. This is a waste of my time'.

Towards the end of the week, she remarked bitterly that I didn't seem to be grieving or anxious, in fact I seemed fine. Too fine. Trying too hard to impress her with being fine. And if it was so unserious that I could be fine, why did I have to go? What's *that* all about?

This attitude, which felt taunting and cruel and impenetrable, and which she insisted was irreparable, lasted right through the first week.

Aware of her history with her mother, I said I thought that she was very worried that I was completely preoccupied with someone dying or dead in my mind, and so she was terrified of being in my presence – she was afraid that I would need something from her and at the same time that I was hopelessly cut-off from her.

This is a deduction I have made from my experience in the session with her: what I *experience* is an angry cold self-sufficient person who I cannot possibly either help or reach and I base my interpretation on an assumption that I am feeling her feelings.

So, at this point, during this first week back, I was aware that something very difficult was going on, and I understood *her* coldness, self-sufficiency, lack of need for me, as necessary to protect her from anxiety about what *I* was like and despair about my being present but utterly lost to her.

By the next week something had changed. In the following material what I think we can see is how the patient's stance has altered: she is still unreachable, impenetrable, but she is no longer angry, she is coldly triumphant. The material is manifestly about her relationship with someone outside the analysis, a child she agreed to keep in foster care, and it presents a particular object relationship in which one person has everything and the other person is left jealous, envious and useless – and completely abandoned.

I hope to show how something has changed in the analytic relationship in response to the work of the previous week.

On Wednesday, she came in, chatted for a while in a cold and distant voice, and then announced that she had decided that in the summer when she and her husband go away, she would get pregnant. She has decided: she will get pregnant. Her only worry she says is whether the council will continue to allow her to foster children since she will have to give Thomas back sooner than she'd agreed. (Thomas, a deeply troubled 4-year-old, had recently come to live with the family as he awaited a more permanent adoption. I had heard a lot about him for several weeks before I went away: how unlikeable he was, how nasty, jealous and unpleasant. We had understood together how much he reminded her of herself as a small child: unliked, unlikeable, unpopular with children and with grown-ups.)

What struck me first about the pregnancy announcement was its suddenness, its decisiveness, its singlemindedness (we didn't hear what her husband thought about it) and her determination to do this no matter who suffered. She returned to Thomas: 'I suppose it will be tough on him', said very casually. 'Well, too bad.' She laughed without humour. 'I'm certainly not going to organize my life and the life of my family around that monstrous child.'

She went on to describe how she would not tell anyone about her pregnancy until Thomas was well and truly settled so that no one interfered with her taking him on, then announce she was pregnant, try to keep him until Easter, and then he'd have to leave.

And as for Thomas, well he'd just have to get used to the idea that she was pregnant. 'Tough', she said. 'People do'.

I was struck by her ruthlessness and by what felt like deliberate cruelty: she seemed to be relishing the idea of confronting this disturbed and unhappy little boy with her blossoming pregnancy for nine long months. And then leaving him at the end.

But of course this image of her – increasingly needed, increasingly important to him, increasingly pregnant and on the verge of leaving him – replete with cruelty and provoking jealousy and envy and despair – seemed particularly relevant to the current situation between me and my patient.

Listening to her, I had to deal with feeling disturbed by her nonchalance and ruthlessness, and by how worried I felt about Thomas. I was worried about a child who has to watch this cruel performance of fecundity. It took me a few moments to realize that the vulnerable child had been completely split off from her awareness of herself and entirely projected into Thomas. The Thomas she was describing was actually carrying this part of her. You might say that in the session, as she spoke, B was not a vulnerable child watching a felt-to-be-cruelly-unavailable mother; B *was* a cruelly unavailable mother.

I said to her:

> When I came back last week after being away, you felt I was horribly and cruelly full of something; horribly pregnant in a sense, my mind and thoughts occupied by a dead or dying mother. And that I came back and paraded this in front of you – didn't stay away, out of sight, but forced you to know about my state – and made you feel there was no room in my mind for you. And that then I would leave again, prematurely, to attend to this same dead parent. I think this felt impossible to bear. I don't think it feels bearable. I think now you have become this version of me, felt to be pregnant with something which leaves you out, pregnant in a horrible way. And I think you want Thomas to feel as bad as you felt – like a horrible child who no one wants to be with and everyone leaves, full of nothing but jealousy and hatred … and you can be the all-filled-up mother.

She responded in a voice of icy triumph:

> I knew it. Typical. There is nothing I can say to you really: you are one of those psychoanalysts who thinks analysis is infinitely more important than family life or having children. I'm afraid I just don't agree with you. We'll just have to disagree about this.

So, who am I and who is she at this moment? At this moment I don't have children, and, although I have, in fact, just come back from two weeks away looking after my family, I am suddenly a psychoanalyst who thinks analysis is infinitely more important than family life! Neither am I an object of desire for her – she's not really interested in talking to me she tells me. I am not specific and I am interchangeable – I am just 'one of those psychoanalysts …' and moreover one who ridiculously overvalues what I do have – psychoanalysis – which is second rate. And she is someone who doesn't need me. She has *become* a particular version of her mother and her current view of her analyst: cold and triumphant, filled with something called 'family life and children' but 'family life and children' are felt to be used by this sort of analyst or mother simply as weapons, arms in the battle for supremacy and being enviable and desirable. I, like Thomas, have to just watch it. She is the powerful mother; I am the helpless child. This is projective identification – and at this point my job is to try to understand it and contain my feelings about it. I have to be careful not to condescend to her or to retaliate.

On Friday she arrived ten minutes late and started the session by saying she had to leave ten minutes early to pick up her son from school – he is moving on to senior school, it is his last day at his old school.

In the session she talked as if she didn't have a care in the world: she was blasé, brittle, uninterested in looking below the top layer of what she was telling me.

She said it is the last day of term at her son David's school. She is best friends with two women – Ana and Mary – who have children in David's class. She tells me that she and Ana had arranged to take their two boys to supper after school today because the boys will be sad about saying good-bye to their friends. David *is* sad, she says. He complained last night of tummy ache – 'obviously it is psychosomatic' – he says he can't eat sweets. Then last night Mary, the other friend, called to ask what are she and David doing after school because Mary and her child would like to meet up with them. 'So', the patient says, 'What am I supposed to do?' Mary will be so hurt if she says she's made plans with Ana, but if she includes both Mary and Ana they will get uncontrollably jealous – each jealous of the friendship she has with the other. It's impossible; they tear each other to shreds. She stopped suddenly and said, 'I notice you're not saying anything.' This came abruptly at me, and I felt an immediate pressure to respond. I considered what I did think and what I thought I should say, could say.

I said: 'I'm wondering how I can say to you what I am thinking.' I said:

> Yesterday you were having thoughts about going away this summer and getting pregnant, and then you were picturing the effect this would have on a child, on Thomas. You were picturing his distress and imagining his jealousy and while you were thinking about it you didn't mind what he felt – you said 'tough'. Today you are telling me about two women who are jealous and envious and can easily feel torn apart and wanting to tear someone else apart from jealousy, but that you are feeling fine and not in any danger and in fact are the object of all desire.

'Well,' she said, dripping with sarcasm. 'So: I'm not at the front of the queue of jealous people? What a shame! I really *love* feeling like that, you know – I *love* those feelings … I want them every day. If unbearable jealousy is what it is.' She paused. 'You've shifted: last week you were talking about "terror", now you are saying it is unbearable jealousy – that feelings of "I can't have this done to me" leads to a whole upsurge of defences so I don't have to feel vulnerable.' She paused again. 'I do very little feeling vulnerable, sad and hurt.' She paused again. 'I'm just noting that. A bit more with Charles than I used to.' She paused. 'I'm not even thinking about Tom's anniversary on the weekend.' (She is referring to the death three years ago of her brother.) 'I'm not preparing to feel anything. I am quite hard at the moment. Is it to do with you going away? Last year I was more in touch.'

I said I think she feels like her son David: she can't eat anything sweet – she can't have any help which might help her to be more in touch.

Actually, she says she *has* been eating sweets. That's the reason she was late today – there were cakes leftover from the office party. She ate several and made herself late.

I said I wondered what she would do if she had had to feel in a hurry: aware that she was late, with the weekend ahead, particularly this difficult weekend – Tom's anniversary and the last weekend before the summer break.

She said, 'I don't know if I'm unusually cut off or if this is usual. I think there is something I once knew but can't get.' She paused:

> If I changed my mind … and said I want to go somewhere else … feel different in here now … I don't know where that would be … I don't know where I want to go. I remember the first time you went away unexpectedly – everything felt ruined. A terrible rupture. This time: that is something I'm not going to feel. I'm much more grown up. Why should I feel that?

I said, Because there are consequences – because she loses her sense of herself. When she says she doesn't feel connected, she doesn't only mean to me but to herself.

She said 'Yeah'. Pause. Her tone changed:

> I'm amazed – impressed really – by David. He's gone from excited to depleted; from crying to really sad and sick. I believe he is doing the right thing, (in moving to a new school) but there is a cost. Pause. He is lucky because he feels the way he does: the teacher said he is empathic – he identifies with peers. I only ever identified with the teacher. So, I never had any friends, ever.

I think that she was describing what was going on in the session at that very moment. In response to my interpretations – to my being able to think about her and talk to her she has a new and more vulnerable feeling 'If I changed my mind … if I want to go somewhere else …'. There is suddenly the possibility of a mind that can change, a 'somewhere else', a 'feeling different', which there hasn't been for days. This is impressive. But she is not able to stay with this more vulnerable state for long, and she quickly does exactly what she says she always used to do: she identifies with the 'teacher'/analyst. She suddenly becomes someone who is 'impressed by David', who she can look at and judge and interpret – his tummy ache is psychosomatic. She is not going to feel the terrible rupture she is afraid of; instead she is going to be a caricatured version of an analyst – a grown-up – who can look at a child and say 'How good that he's in touch with his feelings!'

I say to her that the trouble is, that because she is so busy being what is her picture of the teacher/analyst – like when she talks about David- it leaves her not feeling together with me and not really feeling herself.

She says, 'I don't mean this rudely, I mean it truthfully – you can talk yourself hoarse, I don't think you'll get through to me today.' There is a short silence. Then she goes on: 'Now I'm feeling depressed. More and more depressed. I have a piano lesson this afternoon, I haven't practised, the children won't be there, I don't like the teacher. But I don't feel like doing anything else either: cleaning the house, doing the garden, or inviting people over.'

'All the usual solutions to feeling depressed.'

'Yeah.'

I said I think she feels depressed also because she is not able at the moment to be in the place she was at the start of the session. A place in which she is not just absolutely not jealous, but also can be the absolute object of desire. She doesn't seem to be able to be that at the moment. She's not sure quite why: maybe because I took it away, or because it didn't work, or it dissipated, but in any case, it isn't a solution and it leaves her depressed.

She said 'If I feel I want … just a little … want you to help me … that I really need you to, then I'll completely fall to pieces. There isn't enough time. You'll have to say what you've said all over again.'

I said I thought she is aware all of a sudden of her plan to leave her session early today. I said it seemed to me that although it may be for good reasons: not to be late to pick up children from school, that it had also been co-opted to be part of this same thing that we've been talking about – part of her being the busy object of desire, with me left waiting and alone. And that now it's the end of the session and maybe she suddenly feels this plan has left her with not enough time.

'Mm', she continued:

> Wanting to be the most popular girl. It's so weird. I so wasn't that. I was so unpopular and cruel to other children. I was like Thomas. He sometimes seems to really want to be close to me. But then he mocks me for what he calls my "air holes" – my nostrils. He says they are disgusting. I was just like that: I hated everything about horrible unpopular children: bodies, skin, teeth – I thought it was all disgusting …

I said: air holes are to breathe through. Needing to breathe, needing air, seems disgusting to someone who needs to believe she doesn't need anything. Needing is mockable and detestable. I said that for a moment she was very aware of not wanting to leave her session, of wanting more time, wanting me to say it all again to her. But then she is confronted by a her who thinks such needs are pathetic and disgusting.

The session ended here.

I want to go back over this material briefly to clarify the process I think was going on.

In the first week after my return the patient was pointedly cruel – cold, unreachable and explicitly aggressive. I thought that her aggression was a defence against a terror of being with me, linked in her mind to her mother, felt to be totally occupied by dead and persecuting parents – an object felt to be cruelly unavailable to her and instead needing endless care and concern. In that first week she was in projective identification with just such a cruelly unavailable object – an object possessed by its own persecuting internal object – and she was quite terrifying. I'll call this the first projective identification.

Thinking later about these sessions, I think that my being able to struggle with my own feelings about her cruelty, and to put together in my own mind what I was feeling and what I know about her, and then to show her how I was thinking about her (for example the interpretation that began 'I am wondering how to say to you what I am thinking …') led to a change. I think she felt aware that I was able to hold her in my mind and to digest her experience. 'I am wondering how to say to you …' implies all sorts of things: a mind that isn't frozen, that can wonder, that is taking care of her, that is considering her, that can refer to and hold onto other objects and other feelings but also hold on to her. It is not a mind completely occupied by a dead object of its own.

The following week – as the sessions I've just described demonstrate –something had shifted. Following the work we had done, she no longer feared that I was entirely preoccupied with dead internal objects. Instead, she felt me able to think – about her and thus, of course, about other people in my life – internal figures and external ones. At this point the threat – less dangerous but still unbearable to her – is that she will feel jealous. The jealousy is about people she believes I think about – objects felt to be alive either in reality or in my mind – and the focus of my attention, still to the exclusion of all else. It is *this* version of me – now felt to contain all kinds of good alive things – helpful thoughts, interpretations, lively relationships, who she now *becomes* in projective identification. And once she has become this (enviously and jealously perceived) 'helpful' figure, she can make interpretations about her son's psychosomatic symptoms and his psychic development, she can swan about, provoking Thomas's passionate jealousy and sense of loss, she can be the most popular girl on the block. This is the second projective identification. And my position is that I must simply watch her and only be able to make contact for seconds…and then lose it. I am the little girl watching the yearned for mother, now cruelly full of everything good for everyone else.

On the other hand, if we look closely, we can see that although she is still in projective identification, still being something other than herself, this second projective identification is with a more benign less malevolent figure than the first, and the process is also beginning to soften, to loosen. We can see all this in the material: On Wednesday she is insisting that she *will* be the pregnant one, and *tough* to anyone else. But gradually this shifts: look back at the passage on the Friday where I've interpreted her projection of jealousy into Ana and Mary, and why. She responds with tremendous sarcasm: 'Oh thanks –so I'm not at the front of the queue of jealous people? I really love feeling like that you know' but then her response slows down, it is full of pauses and increasingly thoughtful, about herself and about me. During the previous week she was cold and hard. Now she is observing herself, *noticing* that she is cold and hard. She is more hesitant, more available. This goes on through the session: her tone changes, her attitude becomes more fluid – she moves from *being* the object of desire and envy, to observing such a wish in herself.

The point I am making is that this process of projective identification is not static. Sometimes it is more rigidly maintained and feels unchanging and unchangeable. But frequently, over time, we can observe changes both in the nature of the object identified with, and in the degree of rigidity with which this identification is maintained.

I will finish by giving you a tiny bit of material from the next session, just before the summer break. She again presented at first as cold and unreachable: 'You think I'm determined to be this way. I think: tough! That's how it is. Get used to it.' Eventually I say to her that it seems to me that one of us gets to be impenetrable and the other one has to be desperate. That these are the only two places that exist, and only one of us can feel one, and the other must feel the other. And that there is no other place to be.

She says 'Yes', very quietly and then starts to cry. 'That's right', she says, and then, 'As soon as I feel a tiny bit warmer, that I want to hear what you say, I feel desperate about how little time there is left and how much I've lost.'

She went on:

> There's a fantasy I've had all of a sudden – it seems funny: I wondered, why isn't there a bar on the bed [she means the couch] – a side, so nothing … falls out? Then I thought when psychoanalysis began they probably didn't have that kind of bed. But I don't like the wall here [she touches the wall on her other side] … it keeps me in.

She laughed.

I said she wants a bar that will let her feel she is kept safely in my mind, protected, with room for her, not falling out of my mind but also not locking her into my mind. I thought the wall she doesn't like is both feeling walled out of my mind when she thinks my mind is completely full with no room for her, and, paradoxically, being walled within my mind, when she feels trapped in the presence of a frighteningly depressed me.

She said yes.

At this moment the patient is not in projective identification with one or another malevolent or benign version of her analyst. She is herself, a self of course containing multiple identifications with multiple versions of her objects. But I would suggest that at this point the identifications are more mobile, more fluid and flexible, less rigidly maintained. The objects she identifies with have air holes, bars but not walls.

Reference

Klein, M. (1946) Notes on Some Schizoid Mechanisms. *International Journal of Psychoanalysis* 27: 99–110.

3 Being True to a False Object

A View of Identification

Priscilla Roth

The clinical situation I wish to discuss concerns a group of patients who in some respects resemble Helene Deutsch's (1942) 'as-if' personalities. These are patients who are often highly intelligent and can be high achievers in their professional field, but whose emotional life appears to lack depth and, indeed, often rings false. The patients I am discussing do not appear to be cold; in fact, a kind of overblown emotionality is part of the picture, but it does not feel genuine and has a kind of inappropriate effusiveness: there is a saccharine overcompliance, and little believable warmth. In this sense what feels particularly disturbing to the analyst (and usually to other people in such a patient's life) is the way the most valuable and precious human emotions seem to be parodied and made tawdry: these patients talk a great deal about 'loving feelings' or 'meaningful experiences' or, at other times, 'angry feelings', but the analyst finds it impossible to empathize or indeed believe in such experiences. This is painful for the analyst; I discuss this further at a later point in the chapter.

Following Deutsch, Riesenberg Malcolm (1990) has described the 'as-if' quality of these patients' response to the analytic situation and believes that such patients develop a false structure that she says is 'based on a falsely idealized object. It is doubly false, not only because excessive idealization falsifies, but also because of the object's own pathology' (p. 385)

In this chapter I want to suggest that the falseness, apparent shallowness, and 'as-if' qualities in some of these patients have to do with the presence of these qualities in each patient's original objects, and that their presence in the patient comes about through an identification with this primary object. In analysis it gradually emerges that the patient perceives the primary object not only to have been false but also to have been utterly dependent on its illusions of goodness being maintained. Splitting and idealization are the predominant mechanisms used by such patients, and are directly related to maintaining some link with a good object – that is, they form part of a manic defence against the depression that would arise if they were to have insight into the real nature of the object.

I further suggest that the idealization and the identification can be seen to increase at the moment that the picture of the object is threatened by the

DOI: 10.4324/9781003588870-5

patient's perception of the object's failure, or by disappointment in the object – that is, at the moment when the patient is confronted with new, potentially disturbing perceptions of the object. For such a patient it is the insistence on the 'goodness' of a false idealized object, and the patient's identification with this object, that gives the patient a strange, unattractive quality.

One patient who falls into this category is a young woman in her early thirties who is a well-respected university lecturer, married with three small children. She came to analysis ostensibly because she became interested in applying psychoanalytic concepts to the study of a particular area of academic interest. She is thus extremely well read in psychoanalytic literature and is, as well, a highly intelligent, well-educated and successful woman, recognized in her field as ambitious, clever, energetic and dedicated.

Although her original reasons for seeking analysis were professional, it quickly became clear that something else was being sought. The patient was caught up in all kinds of activities that had made her something of an authority in her field, and she felt pleased and grateful for what seemed to be a meaningful marriage. Still, she had a strange sense that things were not all right, although in ways she could not understand or verbalize. When she did try to put into words what felt wrong, she could only do so in acutely clumsy psychoanalytic jargon: 'I attack my good objects', or 'My envy interferes with my being able to value what is genuinely good'. I felt that these descriptions were more a manifestation of the problem than a description, that while she was trying to communicate something to me by the words she was using, I felt she was conveying something very much more important by the style and manner of her communication. There was a hollowness to the description that felt false and also sad, and I came to feel that this young woman did not really know how she felt or how to begin to attend to or describe her own feelings. I thought she did not have any clear idea of the difference between what she actually felt and what she thought she was supposed to feel.

My sadness listening to her was even more acute because she clearly did not feel sad. Indeed, she was known among her colleagues at the university as endlessly cheerful, positive, energetic and optimistic – she was sometimes, in fact, teased about this. She told me early on that as a child she had read a story about a Buddhist monk who was so loathe to hurt any living thing that he walked around barefoot all his life in order not to kill any insects he might tread on. For many years she had modelled herself on this monk, as well as on a character in a television series whose most distinctive characteristics were her cheerful smile and her proud insistence that she had never been deliberately cruel to anyone in her life.

The patient comes from a tightly knit Italian family that emigrated to England in her grandparents' generation but that still retains strong links with Italy. The patient was very involved with her family until the moment of her marriage, when her husband helped her to 'realize how disturbed [her] parents were'. My impression is that from that time, she abruptly shifted allegiances, and transferred her idealization from her parents to her new husband.

At the time her analysis began, she described her mother as slatternly, intrusive, dirty, inappropriately sexual (for example, disturbingly interested in the patient's breasts and salaciously commenting on the sexiness of a teenage niece) and frequently bizarre. The father, a less vividly described character, is seen as doting on the mother, full of a kind of overblown sentimentality, and joining with the mother in an arrogant disregard for what is labelled 'bourgeois' order and cleanliness.

My patient describes her parents' home as 'filthy' – all areas of the house covered in dirty dishes, full ashtrays, old bits of food, as well as books and papers – with the parents blissfully insisting they have more important things to attend to than housekeeping.

The parents both work for a large charity organization concerned with encouraging international goodwill and attempting to meet the needs of people in Third World countries. Every holiday the family invites homeless people from an underdeveloped country to spend the holiday with them. In pursuing their work the parents travelled a great deal; my patient and her younger sisters were never in any one school longer than eighteen months. When she describes her parents she gives a picture of a cloying, intrusive, self-righteous couple. Her husband, on the other hand, is presented as clear-thinking, morally impeccable, consistently fair, and justified in even the most autocratic and tyrannical behaviour. In the analysis I very quickly took on all the characteristics of the husband – everything I said was felt to be right, and everything I did was defended as correct. This extended to my being late for a session, and my making a mistake on her bill.

In the early months of her analysis, my patient spoke fluently and brought what should have been absorbing material about her quite remarkable childhood, her family history, and current events in her life. She listened attentively when I spoke, and agreed with most of my comments. I found myself becoming increasingly bored and irritated. She was clearly not 'thrown' by anything I said; indeed, she absorbed all my interpretations and suggestions and immediately brought evidence to support them.

But it all felt phony and lifeless. The material she brought, which was so rich on the surface, also felt lifeless and forced. She described events in her childhood with a kind of platitudinous monotony, even though she used images that should have been powerful. She would refer, for instance, to her mother's 'knitting-needle abortion', but in a way that made it feel like a cliché. This abortion, which took place when my patient was four years old, was referred to dozens of times in the first months, as was her mother's miscarriage of another baby because she went cycling 'though the doctor told her not to', and the fact that the patient 'went to fifteen schools in fourteen years'. All these events were only, though repeatedly, inserted as dependent clauses in the middle of sentences ostensibly about something else. Thus, the patient would say:

The dress in the dream reminds me of a dress I wore in the school in Edinburgh when I was about four, which is where we lived when my mother had the knitting-needle abortion, and I wore it to a birthday party of a friend.

During the first months I considered such statements from many different angles; I gradually came to feel that certain events in her life had been labelled 'traumatic', and that although many of them might well have been traumatic, labelling them had replaced experiencing or knowing about them. And I was aware that something false happened in the analysis if we simply addressed these events. It was only when I was able to speak with her about how difficult it was for her to know what she actually felt about any of these experiences, including telling me about them, that I felt something more alive taking place for a moment in the session.

I thought that all these events in her past and in her present had become clichés, and the telling of them was clichéd, and I felt I was in danger of becoming a cliché, too: an analyst listening to pre-digested stories and making utterly predictable interpretations about them. And I felt we were in danger of engaging in an 'as-if' analysis: she would bring material, I would interpret it, as if we were a couple in meaningful contact with each other. Whereas I was feeling repeatedly caught up in something false, my patient was repeatedly telling me how relieved she was to be in such a good analysis with such an excellent analyst (see also Joseph, 1975; Sodré, 1989, Riesenberg Malcolm, 1990).

The material I want to present began towards the end of the first year of her analysis. One day the patient told me that a friend of hers had been at a psychoanalytic conference at which I had been present. There had been a dance one night, and the friend had made a joke that I had probably been dancing with my husband.

The following week the patient dreamed she was at a dance, wearing a dress that was too tight, too short, too youthful. The dress was very low cut and her breasts hung out ludicrously. She was obviously trying to be sexy and attractive but in fact she looked fat, grotesque and old. She was trying to dance, showing off really, but was only able to do dances from twenty years ago, such as the twist.

Her associations to the dream began with a book she had been reading, which described a middle-aged married couple in bed together and spoke about them facing each other in bed 'like two Etruscan statues'. She had thought this was a moving description of the beauty of aging bodies. She thought, then, about her own wedding dress, which had been second-hand – like everything her mother had ever bought her, she said. The fabric was beautiful, but the dress did not fit her. It was someone else's dress, and never felt right on her, although they had had it altered.

I reminded my patient about her friend's comment about my being at a dance, and suggested that her dream seemed connected with that. I thought she had somewhere in her mind a picture of me like the figure who was her in the dream. I thought she could not face this picture of me: dirty, grotesque, disgusting, pretending to be something I wasn't, because it so threatened her need to see me as attractive, believable and trustworthy. I suggested that instead of knowing about this view she had of me, she *became* that version of me, as she did in the dream. I added that in her dream she seemed to know that she was identified with a me who was felt to be a sham – that in the dream she was all dressed up pretending to be something, but she knew it was a pretence. In her associations, however, she backed away from what she knew: she idealized 'aging bodies', which are like 'Etruscan statues' in bed; in her dream the aging body, caught up in a desperate attempt at sexuality, was 'fat, grotesque and old'.

She then told me that in fact she likes to dance very much but that her husband hates dancing and hates to see her dance, because he feels it is like having sexual intercourse in public.

I said I thought when she was forced, by her friend's information, to think of my husband and me dancing, it felt to her like being forced to watch a kind of public intercourse – and that this felt dirty and grotesque – but that it got idealized into Etruscan statues while she herself, in the dream, became grotesque and hateful. There was an indication that she *knew* that this image did not belong to her in the first place – that in the first place it was a picture in her mind of *my* marriage – it was a 'second-hand wedding dress' she was putting on.

My patient seemed to understand quite easily what I was saying, and to see that it made sense, but said that of course she found it impossible to imagine thinking such things about me.

In the next session the patient returned to the subject of her dream and how difficult it was for her to believe that she had such thoughts about me. I found myself trying to show her the enormous contrast between the picture of me that exists in her conscious mind – sane, organized, appropriate, wise, attractive and intelligent – and her repeated and insistent descriptions of her mother – filthy, disorganized, emotionally dishonest and unable to think clearly. But in my attempts to show this to the patient I did not want to use the word 'split' because I was afraid of the patient's capacity to turn everything into 'psychobabble' or 'psychoanalese' and not to be fresh and specific. So, in a clumsy and probably misguided attempt to avoid this problem, and in the heat of the moment of making an interpretation, I used the word 'fissure' where 'split' was the obvious word to use. So, I said something like, 'I think you make an enormous … [pause] … fissure … between your picture of me and your picture of your mother, and keep us very far apart in your mind.'

What happened next was very interesting. The patient immediately adopted the word 'fissure' and over the next few sessions used it to describe all kinds of situations. She would say, 'I think my husband makes a fissure between me and my sister', or 'I can see the way I make a fissure between those things I want to know about myself and those things I can't let myself know.'

Now, we are all familiar with the way some patients take hold of our words and use them as things – to hold on to, to get inside of – rather than using them to understand an idea which we are trying to communicate. What was happening here included much of this, but had something else besides (and this is the point I want to stress); I think my patient was very aware, although not quite consciously, of my discomfort and clumsiness, and of the inappropriateness both of the word 'fissure' and of my awkward, bumbling manner. I think she could not acknowledge this to me, nor, much more importantly, to herself. Much less could she acknowledge how contemptuous and triumphant it made her feel. Feelings of triumph and contempt towards the analyst are uncomfortable for most patients; when they are provoked by something the analyst actually does they are particularly uncomfortable. What I want to emphasize, however, is that for some patients, like the woman I am describing, such feelings are dealt with by *immediate denial*, and the very behaviour or quality that is felt to be wrong, a disappointment in or a failure of the analyst, is idealized and identified with.

I am suggesting that these particular patients spend their lives avoiding an awareness of the actual nature of their objects. They are terrified of discovering the falseness of the object: it is not that the object itself is bad; it is much more that its goodness is false, unreal, unbelievable, and a corruption of genuine goodness.

For such people, something has gone awry with the establishment of strong, essentially solid internal objects. In 'Some Theoretical Conclusions Regarding the Emotional Life of the Infant', Klein (1952), while discussing the development from the paranoid-schizoid to the depressive position, wrote:

> Steps in integration characteristic of the period when the infant is negotiating the depressive position result in a greater capacity of the ego to acknowledge the increasingly poignant psychic reality. The anxiety relating to the internalized mother who is felt to be injured, suffering, in danger of being annihilated or already annihilated and lost forever, leads to a stronger identification with the injured object. This identification reinforces both the drive to make reparation and the ego's attempts to inhibit aggressive impulses. The ego also again and again makes use of the manic defence... denial, idealization, splitting and control of internal and external objects are used by the ego to counteract persecutory anxiety. These omnipotent methods are maintained when the depressive position arises but they are now predominantly used to counteract depressive anxiety. They also undergo changes, in keeping with the steps in integration and synthesis, that is to say they become less extreme and correspond more to the growing capacity of the ego to face psychic reality. With this later form and aim these early methods now constitute the manic defence ... There is also a difference in the use of splitting the object and the self. The ego ... now divides the complete object into an uninjured live object and an

injured and endangered one: splitting thus becomes largely a defence against depressive anxiety ... his capacity for dealing with (depressive) anxiety is to some degree determined by his earlier development ... by the extent to which he has been able to take in and establish his good object which forms the core of his ego.

(Klein, 1952, pp. 212–216; emphasis added)

The concept of identification has grown in importance in psychoanalytic theory since its earliest uses by Freud, beginning with his 'On Narcissism' (Freud, 1914) and 'Mourning and Melancholia' (Freud, 1917). Identification has become, as Laplanche and Pontalis (1967) point out, 'not simply one psychical mechanism among others, but the operation itself whereby the human subject is constituted' (p. 206). In the passage quoted, Klein is describing the process by which the infant not only *introjects* good objects so that they are, in Sandler's (1988) definition, 'unconscious, internal "phantom" companions, felt to be part of one's inner world, yet external to one's self-representation', but also *identifies with* these objects, so that they 'form the core of his ego' itself (p. 11).

Introjection and identification are complicated mechanisms at all times, and are always affected by projective processes. Much of the time with our patients we are dealing with the way projection and projective identification alter and affect their internal and external objects. This is also true for the patients I am describing. In this chapter, however, I am focusing on a different problem. I am suggesting that for some patients the presence of a kind of shallow falseness, this gushy saccharine quality I have described in my patient, is the result of an identification with a primary object who was perceived as false, but who appears to have been dependent on the falseness never being identified and recognized as such.

The problem for these patients is how to deal with the falseness of the object, when the false object is the closest thing to a good object that is available. In this situation, and desperate to hold on to the good object, the patient resorts to massive splitting and idealization. It is not, here, a question of the ordinary, and reasonably fluid splitting that often forms part of normal and necessary manic attempts to deal with depressive anxieties as they arise. For my patient, an impenetrable manic defence of splitting, denial, and idealization became fixed into a characterological organization, which Steiner (1987) has described as a 'pathological organization'. This firmly fixed manic structure threatens her with dangerous feelings of contempt, triumph, and the need to control. She splits her object into a hated, contemptible object (my patient's view of her mother) while preserving and protecting an idealized object who is never allowed to be open to criticism or fallible (my patient's view of her husband and of her analyst). The splitting and idealization come into play because they are her predominant defences against the depression that would arise if she were to have some real insight into the nature of her object.

In my patient's dream, in which she wears the too-tight dress at the dance and is presenting herself as something she is not, I think she is aware of being identified with an analyst who she feels is false. I am not suggesting that I was actually false on this occasion; I am suggesting that I was felt to be false in terms of the dream – needing to be seen as young, sexy, attractive, desirable – to conceal from myself my real, much less attractive qualities. I am also suggesting that my patient may well perceive moments of anxiety or disturbance in me that become part of her picture of a false, fragile analyst. The point is not whether such moments of anxiety or disturbance (hopefully minor) are present – they exist in all analysts and in all analyses. The point is for the analyst to be acutely aware of them, and of what their consequences are in the patient.

Sohn (1985) has written about how some patients can show much more insight into their own psychic reality in their dreams than they can when they are awake; this patient's dream and associations are an example of that phenomenon. In the dream there is the insight: 'My mother/analyst presents herself as beautiful and desirable but is actually grotesque and bizarre, and I dress up to be like her and become equally bizarre.' This insight is all but lost in the session, when once again the analyst's/mother's aging body is idealized and parental intercourse is not the grotesque twisted farce of the dream but is two Etruscan statues, coolly facing each other in the beauty of middle-aged love.

My patient's idealization of and identification with her object increase at the very moment that the object is threatened with being perceived as fraudulent. This is what happened with the 'fissure' incident. Actually, to have a new perception about her object would require a narrowing of the split she has made between the despised object and the idealized object. This is not possible for my patient because her good object is so falsely constructed that to take away its ideal quality would be felt to leave it hopelessly exposed.

Viewing the object realistically would also mean a tremendous narcissistic loss. This is because so much of the patient's self has been projected into this idealized object that disappointment in (and therefore loss of) this object means for the patient a loss of parts of herself as well as a loss of her good internal object.

It is out of the need to prevent such catastrophic loss that these patients identify with false idealized objects and insist on their 'goodness', and it is this identification that gives these patients such strange, unattractive qualities. When I use the word 'fissure' instead of the more obvious 'split' I am presenting myself as smoothly in control, but I have actually been clumsy and a little bit ridiculous. My patient cannot bear this and cannot bear the danger I am in if she knows about her contempt and triumph when I am ridiculous. She immediately idealizes my ridiculousness and identifies with it.

It is a commonplace to note that we can never know what our patients' original objects were like in reality. I would guess that my patient's mother was desperately afraid to look at her own shattered internal world, and that the facade of 'goodness' she wore was necessary for her own equilibrium. I get this impression from what my patient tells me about her mother and from the way her idealization of me seems to repeat an earlier idealization of her mother. But I suggest that the real evidence I have about my patient's original object comes from the strength of the patient's response to my actual insincerity. In the dream, when the patient identifies with me as grotesquely false, she is, I think, identifying with a picture of me altered by her hatred, envy and jealousy. This identification remains in the dream, and within the dream she is able to know something about it. This is, I suggest, in contrast to what happens in the session when I am in fact false – when I use an overblown, somewhat pretentious word where a much simpler one would do. On this occasion she becomes false and insincere in her identification with me, and there seems to be no part of her available to recognize this. In other words, I suggest that the magnitude of the patient's response to this actual falseness in her present object, may give us a particular kind of information about the nature of her objects in the past.

Another patient who was of this same type described how her mother prided herself on being 'open' and 'non-neurotic', and used to sit on the toilet and defecate with the lavatory door purposely left wide open to demonstrate her 'openness'. This patient often spoke to me of her own 'warm, loving feelings' towards me, while simultaneously holding under nose in a wad of crumpled-up toilet paper and then examining the contents close enough to me for me to have to either close my eyes or examine them as well! It was only when I understood how disturbing it was to be expected to 'love' someone who was disgusting me, that I was able to talk to the patient about her own experience in a way that made contact with her.

In her article 'Can a Liar Be Psychoanalysed?' O'Shaughnessy (1990) suggests that habitual liars lie because they are in identification with a lying object. Kernberg (1992, p.10) has made a similar point. Following Klein and Bion, O'Shaughnessy maintains that an infant has an innate preconception of a good object that will meet the infant's needs for food, warmth and comfort; and who will take in and understand the infant's communications. When the infant's experience does not correspond sufficiently to his expectations, 'the infant may doubt if the object is a true realization of his innate preconception' (O'Shaughnessy, 1990, p. 90). That is, the infant, from a very early age, may have some perception of the falseness of the object – its essential inadequacies, combined with a false facade of adequacy. O'Shaughnessy sees the disturbance of the lying patient as 'a malformation of the paranoid-schizoid position, when normally an infant polarizes his experiences into good and bad. [The infant whose primary object is a liar], however, lacks good objects, and splits instead between suspect object and bad objects' (O'Shaughnessy, 1990, p. 191). The disturbance of these patients is greatly exacerbated by the intensity of their infantile anxiety and hostility, as well as by the way they are able to eroticize the false, lying relationship.

The patients I am describing have something in common with, but are also clearly different from, the habitual liars O'Shaughnessy writes about. They do not deliberately lie, and they do not consciously obfuscate. It is my impression that they get much less pleasure from their falseness than do habitual liars. I suggest that the patients I am discussing, whose falseness has to do with a lack of genuineness, have developed further into the depressive position than liars. That is, I think they can better tolerate the actual goodness of their objects when it arises. The patients' anxiety seems to centre much more on preserving their objects from the effects of the patients' accurate perceptions as well as from their destructive phantasies. On the other hand, the hold these patients have on the depressive position is tenuous, and behind the fear of the loss of the good (idealized) object is always the terror of falling into a much more primitive, fragmented state of mind. The fear of such a regression adds to the tenacity with which these patients cling to and insist on the object's perfection.

References

Deutsch, H. (1942) Some Forms of Emotional Disturbances and their Relationship to Schizophrenia. *Psychoanalytic Quarterly* 11: 301–321.

Freud, S. (1914) On Narcissism. In J. Strachey (ed.), *The Standard Edition of the Complete Psychological Works of Sigmund Freud*, vol. 14 (pp. 73–102). London: Hogarth Press [1957].

Freud, S. (1917) Mourning and Melancholia. In J. Strachey (ed.), *The Standard Edition of the Complete Psychological Works of Sigmund Freud*, vol. 14 (pp. 243–258). London: Hogarth Press [1957].

Joseph, B. (1975) The Patient Who Is Difficult to Reach. In P. L. Giovancchini (ed.), *Tactics and Techniques in Psychoanalytic Therapy*, vol. 2 (pp. 205–216). New York: Aronson.

Kernberg, O. (1992) Psychoanalytic Psychotherapy with Borderline Patients. Presented at the conference on The Psychoanalytic Approach to Borderline States, organized by the University College, Psychoanalysis Unit, London, 24–25 January.

Klein, M. (1952) Some Theoretical Conclusions Regarding the Emotional Life of the Infant. In: *Developments in Psycho-analysis*, ed. J. Rivière. London: Hogarth Press.

Laplanche, J. & Pontalis, J. B. (1967) *The Language of Psychoanalysis*, trans. D. Nicholson-Smith. New York: Norton [1973].

O'Shaughnessy, E. (1990) Can a Liar Be Psychoanalysed? *International Journal of Psycho-analysis* 71: 187–195.

Riesenberg Malcolm, R. (1990) As-If: The Phenomenon of Not Learning. *International Journal of Psycho-analysis* 71: 385–392.

Sandler, J. (1988) *Projection, Identification, Projective Identification*. London: Karnac.

Sodré, I. (1989) Transference Alliances: Therapeutic and Anti-therapeutic. Presented to English Speaking Conference, London.

Sohn, L. (1985) Narcissistic Organization, Projective Identification, and the Formation of the Identificate. *International Journal of Psycho-analysis* 66: 201–213.

Steiner, J. (1987) The Interplay between Pathological Organizations and the Paranoid-Schizoid and Depressive Positions. *International Journal of Psycho-analysis* 68: 69–80.

4 Absolute Zero

A Man Who Doubts His Own Love ...

Priscilla Roth

Fundamental to Kleinian thought is the belief that the early ego coheres around its experiences of a good object. This is the beginning of psychic structure. The first organization and the integration of the ego depend on experiences in which 'Good' (= Me, made up of Good Me/Good object), can be differentiated and separated from 'Bad' (= Not Me, made up of Bad me/Bad object). This earliest structuring is essential; without it, or when it collapses, we assume the infant feels itself to be disintegrating, fragmented, incoherent.

Later on in development, the presence of the internal good object, now more solidly installed within the ego, with less rigidity and less splitting – that is, with more recognition of its own real qualities, good and bad – remains essential. The richness of life, the flexibility of personality, the capacity to face difficulties, all of these are dependent on the experience that one is loved by one's good objects within oneself. Indeed, the sense of having a psychic structure is a sense of being loved, held and integrated by good figures within. If this sense disappears, even for a moment, that moment is catastrophic.

In this chapter I want to discuss two different phenomena, frequently observed, which are connected with the experience of the loss of the good internal object.

First, I want to focus on a particular aspect of melancholic depression: that in such states of mind, the presence of the bad object in the mind is absolute. What I mean is that what is destroyed in depression is not only present peace of mind, but any belief in past experiences of goodness. Indeed, one of the hallmarks of this state is a conviction that any previous sense of well-being was false and self-deluding. The feeling is that one always, in fact, knew one was no good, and now can no longer pretend to believe one has any goodness. History itself is transformed and everything that one is, or ever has been, is either hopelessly bad, or pathetically insufficient to offer any succour against one's badness.

The experience of feeling abandoned by one's internal objects is universal – everyone is capable of falling into this kind of state under sufficient internal or external pressure. But some people feel particularly prey to this

DOI: 10.4324/9781003588870-6

sense of catastrophic internal threat, and construct psychological organizations specifically designed to deny its existence.

It is in the light of this aspect of depression – the absoluteness of the loss of a good internal object – that I want to look at a particular kind of experience which can occur within an analysis.

The experience I mean occurs when, in the course of an analysis which seems to be proceeding reasonably well, and usually in response to an interpretation felt by the analyst to be merely a continuation of work which has already been done, and therefore digestible and thinkable about by the patient, suddenly the patient instead responds to the interpretation with a mixture of rage and terror: rage at the analyst for saying – more importantly, for thinking -such a thing about him – and terror because, from his point of view, the only object who exists is one who hates him: suddenly the whole analytic relationship is in serious, even dire jeopardy. From the analyst's point of view, the degree and the quality of the patient's sudden distress come as a shock; what seems most shocking is that while this is going on, the patient has no believable memory of an analyst with whom, the moment before, he felt he had a helpful, fundamentally benign relationship. (As in depression, the loss of the good object is absolute.) It is not simply that the analyst is felt to be wrong, to have misunderstood or to have been unfair – it is rather that the analyst has suddenly become absolutely bad, and no memory of her having been ever felt to have been good is available to modify the situation. It is the qualities of surprise and violence which make the disappearance of anything good seem so shocking.

My point is that this is anger of a special quality. What has happened feels cataclysmic. It is a terrifying state. The patient feels internally and externally attacked to such an extent that he feels his survival depends on his somehow escaping from what feels like a profoundly threatening experience. It is very important not to underestimate this terror. Freud made it clear that for the self to survive, it needs to feel loved by its internal objects: 'To the ego, living means the same as being loved … by the super-ego' (Freud 1923, p. 58); a patient at such a moment has lost the sense of being loved by anything inside himself.

But this situation is also frightening for the analyst, because the patient, in order to protect himself against the sense of being attacked so powerfully without and within, reverses the situation, and turns on the analyst, who is then established as unforgivably, irredeemably bad. In fact, what the patient does is to introjectively identify with a hateful, rejecting object, and, by means of projective identification, to violently expel feelings of unworthiness into the analyst. The analyst now experiences that same state of mind that her patient was in a moment before: she believes she is bad, and is alone with a patient who has turned completely against her. It is now the analyst who experiences the distress of being left helplessly at the mercy of a hateful, attacking object.

The patient's response is, of course, a paranoid response. In the face of an overwhelming threat to his equilibrium, a patient who, until that moment, was in the depressive position, has moved into the paranoid-schizoid posi-tion: the manic defences have suddenly failed, he is faced with a massive threat and he responds with paranoid mechanisms. Segal (1981) describes the way that, 'Throughout his lifetime an individual oscillates between a paranoid-schizoid and a depressive internal organization', varying 'in force with each individual psychopathology' (p. 16). She also comments that 'The paranoid-schizoid and depressive positions are not only stages of develop-ment. They are two types of ego integration and organization and the ego has a constant struggle to maintain a state of integration' (Segal, 1981, p. 16).

My point is that in the situation I have described, faced with what feels like the absolute loss of his good object, and the insufficiency of his manic defences to protect him, the patient prevents himself from falling to pieces with paranoid mechanisms.

I have come to feel that these moments are particularly important because they face us with a stark and undisguised picture of the internal world that the patient has been suddenly confronted with, and from which he is so desperately trying to escape. It is a world movingly described by Joan Riviere (1936, p. 313), who speaks of 'the situation in which all one's loved ones within are dead and destroyed, all goodness is ... lost, nothing is left within but utter desolation'.

The feeling that one has been abandoned by one's good internal object is the equivalent of knowing one is bad. One is hated from inside, irredeem-ably, allowed no peace of mind, no sense of internal worth. One's very self is hated, and therefore is hateful. This is what Freud described when he wrote: 'The fear of death in melancholia only admits of one explanation: that the ego gives itself up because it feels itself hated and persecuted by the super-ego, instead of loved' (Freud, 1923, p. 58).

Such a horrific internal state fills the patient with despair, and all his efforts focus on averting his own 'death from despair', by frantic attempts to split off the experience of terror and project it into the analyst. But behind the patient's immediate response, one can perceive more subtle and habitual structures which at one and the same time try to repair and revive his inter-nal world, and to deny its existence. These attempts form themselves into the manic defences.

There are of course many possible causes for such a reaction in the middle of an analysis. I suggest that we can see such reactions in patients who are not very disturbed and yet who have developed an elaborate, subtle and sophisticated manic structure which attempts to protect them from, but in fact leaves them horrifyingly vulnerable to, attacks of overwhelming anxiety about the state of their internal worlds.

There are two important points about such structures. The first is that they are omnipotent. That is, they correspond to Freud's picture of omnipotent phantasies, as described in his 'Formulations on the Two Principles of Mental Functioning' (Freud, 1911); they are elaborate hallucinatory wish-fulfilments, about which thought is impossible. They are unquestioned and unquestionable; from the patient's point of view, they just are. 'So long as a phantasy is omnipotent,' writes Segal (1981, p. 221), 'it is not a thought because it is not recognized as such. When a phantasy is recognized as a product of one's own mind, it moves into the realm of thought.'

(A small boy once said to me, looking thoughtful, 'Does everyone think he's the main guy?' Answering him 'Yes', it occurred to me that from the moment he could pose the question, he had stepped out of the absolute assumption that he was the 'main guy' – it had become a thought that 'everyone' could think.)

The patients I am talking about do not recognize that the phantasy within which they live is a phantasy. And it is the nature of such omnipotent phantasies that, however subtly, they structure the world in such a way as fundamentally to deny the independence, the separateness and the unique importance of the object.

This is the second fundamental point about the manic structures I am discussing – they seek to maintain the narcissistic delusion that the object is actually a part of or an extension of the self. While the phantasy is operative, however subtly, with whatever modifications to take account of reality, it is as if the analyst is a figment of the patient's imagination. As one patient put it to me towards the end of a very difficult working-through of these problems: 'It is as if everyone – my parents, my brothers, my boyfriend, you – were all figures in an elaborate doll's house in my mind … and I could just move everyone around to where I decided they were.'

While the phantasy is maintained and not threatened, it feeds on itself, and it can go on and on forever. It can get support from, and misuse, the healthier parts of the patient, and the real therapeutic alliance. This is why it is so shocking when it collapses.

Many writers (particularly Segal, Klein, Deutsch, Riviere) have described the manic defence in detail. I want to emphasize here what it is defensive against, and the subtle way it can be used within analysis.

There is a particular kind of contempt which such patients make use of, nearly invisible to both patient and analyst, which has the effect of eating away at the position of the analyst in the patient's mind. It is a kind of chronic, mild contempt, and it often presents itself as no more than an easy sense of humour or a mild, appropriately sceptical attitude to analysis. The patient seems to assume that it is a perfectly acceptable, even unavoidable way to feel about his analyst: he has a kind of 'yeah, yeah' or 'blah blah blah' attitude to interpretations about things called 'weekends' or 'my husband' or 'the other patients'. These concepts all exist in inverted commas for him – he doesn't really believe in them, and, much more insidious, he doesn't think the analyst really believes in them either. It is a condescending and corrosive attitude; most dangerous of all, it is finally corrosive of the patient's belief in his capacity to love. The corrosiveness is circular and devastating: our survival depends on being loved by our good internal objects; but our internal objects are entirely dependent on our love for them in order for them to survive. Treating one's objects with secret contempt leaves one with a terrible sense that one is only pretending to love, that there is nothing trustworthy or genuinely loving about oneself, and that therefore there is nothing trustworthy or loving about one's objects. 'A man who doubts his own love may, or rather *must*, doubt every lesser thing', wrote Freud (1909, p. 241).

For if the patient's phantasy of a relationship with a narcissistically perceived idealized object, a phantasy which simultaneously keeps the actual object in contempt, and allows him to maintain his view of himself as loving and appreciative is all-pervasive, it is also, paradoxically, not really believed in.

The patient actually knows, underneath, that the world he has created is not only false and deceitful; above all, it is fragile. He feels he is a fraud, and that he is gambling that he won't ever have actually to face what goes on inside him, and what he does to his objects by his secretly contemptuous attitude towards them. He suspects that all his efforts to create a sense of meaning are just pretence – he feels that he is a sham, but he feels hopeless about being able to be otherwise, and thinks that the best he can hope for is to hold off some final reckoning of how things are. He has made a kind of deal – he placates, appeases, manipulates, buys off his objects; bargains with them – to keep at bay the knowledge of who he is, and the empty, fraudulent state of his internal world. One day, he tells himself, he'll sort it out ... or perhaps not ... perhaps he can get by after all.

And this is why the goodness of the object disappears so completely at moments such as those I have described which suddenly occur in the middle of the analysis. The trust in his objects' love for him, and his love for them, which is at base one and the same thing, disappears because it was never really believed in, never really established. Now the patient is confronted with the fragility of the structure he has been hoping would see him through, and the internal state of affairs behind that fragile structure.

At such moments, confronted by a patient who now perceives her as entirely bad, and with her own feelings of loneliness and doubts about herself, the analyst is under great pressure to restore the situation to the *status quo ante* – to restore a sense of mutual well- being between herself and her patient. I think these moments of rupture should serve to make us hesitate before we try to get back to the more comfortable situation.

At the time of which I am speaking, the patient was in his early thirties – an American lawyer, he had come to London to work for an international organization which involved itself with penal reform. He came to analysis because he was suffering some often quite acute depression and some periods of panic following the breakup of his marriage shortly before he left America. Intelligent, nice looking, and likable, he quickly became involved in his analysis; he spoke easily about his past, his family and his current life, and seemed relieved to be in analysis. But something happened early on which caught my attention: on a Friday towards the end of the second month, the patient complained about his flatmate wanting to have separate stockpiles of food, and his fury at this: why couldn't they share every-thing? If they were going to share the flat, why not share the food, too? It was not a question of his not wanting to pay his share, he just didn't understand why there ought to be two lots of food! I interpreted this as his indignation about the coming weekend, tying it in with some material about the flatmate himself. On the Monday the patient reported that things were much better with the flat-mate, that it had been a big help just coming and talking to me on Friday – it feels good that I listen to him. I said I thought he was leaving something out, that I thought he had felt better not just because I had listened but because I had said some things to him which had seemed to sort some things out, and I con-nected this with the Friday sharing-the-food material. He became fur-ious – what on earth was I talking about? I couldn't bear his having sorted something out himself, I was being an 'analyst'! Doing my 'ana-lytic thing', just as he'd suspected I would. He is not at all sure he wanted this analysis after all!

I was immediately aware that everything about him had hardened towards me. I thought this was a different picture of this man than I had previously been aware of, and that I would need to be on the lookout for what this was about. At the end of the session, he left in a rage.

In the event, things settled down and the analysis was taking its course. The period I want to focus on came in the second and third years of the analysis. The patient was working hard to communicate his experiences and to understand what was going on. He came to a Monday session reporting that all weekend he had wanted to come back because he wanted to clarify things he had said – correct what he thought was my view of what he was saying. He was preoccupied the whole weekend with what I must have thought about what he'd said on the Friday, and he had actu-ally had the thought to phone me Sunday to clarify and correct my views ... luckily he'd stopped himself just in time! He then spoke about going back to America for Thanksgiving. He would be seeing old friends – ordinarily he wouldn't have worried about it, but he now feels it is all bound up with his analysis – he'll have to be thinking the whole time about what I would think of them: what if he disagrees with them, or what if he likes them and thinks I would disagree with them.

I suggested that he felt afraid about what I would be thinking about him on the weekend; this had made him anxious. He wanted to rush back to correct and control what I was thinking, to make sure he didn't have to worry about what I think. I thought that he was afraid that he would somehow 'go bad' in my mind. I went on to say that he wouldn't be able to just speak to his friends in America, because he's afraid both about what bad things I would be thinking about him and them, and what bad things he and they might think about me. He is terrified that when he goes away something bad will happen to me in his mind, and to him in mine.

He agreed with this, and then suddenly remembered a dream from the weekend:

> *We are in America together at Thanksgiving dinner. My family was all around the table, mixed up with his family – 'like one big happy family'. He thought how nice it was that I do Thanksgiving just the way his family does ... same foods, same rituals, etc. He noticed that there was a cook in the kitchen, who was doing most of the cooking, and he had the thought that it was very nice that I didn't tire myself out with actually cooking the meal; he was glad I was taking care of myself.*

His associations were that he supposed he wanted us to be the same. And also, that I was much less formal than in the analysis, much friendlier.

(What I was aware of was: (1) that the food was now being 'shared'; and (2) the particular condescension within his pleasure that I didn't tire myself but let someone else do the cooking. I thought in fact this was being played out within the session, and I suspected within the analysis in general, since I thought he was helping me with my understanding, in a way which was true, and helpful, and he meant it, and understood; but which perpetuated the idea that we do everything the same, and that it was very lucky for me that someone else (the patient) was doing the real cooking!)

He came back from the long Christmas break having had a 'terrific' time. He felt I had been in his mind in a very good way during the break; he had felt helped and supported. While in his home city, he had wondered, laughing to himself, whether he would run into me, since he has a pretty good idea I come from the same large city he does. (In fact, this is not true.)

In the middle of the second year he met a girl with whom he became seriously involved; after some 8 months they decided they wanted to marry. He was extremely happy and felt fortunate and grateful. His fiancée was an English woman. One night some American friends of his arrived and he planned a dinner for them to meet the fiancée. He came back the next Monday in very great distress, to tell me that he was not at all sure he was, in fact, in love with her – he thought he had acted too hastily when he'd agreed to marry. He would have to tell her that evening that they would have to end the relationship – he was not really in love with her. He explained that at the dinner with his friends she had been awkward and not a part of the general group atmosphere – she'd in fact been quite boring, he didn't see why he hadn't realized before how boring she is and how he couldn't possibly be with her. He was very distressed about this.

Various things seemed to have happened, including a confusion of his girlfriend with himself, so that he had projected aspects of himself into her. She had become the repository of what was bad and unlovable, and he was now ready to throw her away. She had become not like (the ideal) him; and also not like him-and-me. But what was most striking was how he had 'lost' her; how he had lost any picture of the young woman he loved and valued, and how, instead, she could become completely without lovable qualities in his mind. He had lost his love. When we could understand this as an attack he made on her because of her independence from him, and link this with events within the analysis, he felt relieved and able to resume the relationship.

Another recurring theme in the analysis involved his constantly taking on too much work, over-burdening himself. At first this was mostly to do with his eagerness to help 'his' prisoners, and his insistence that nobody else cared enough to do the job properly. Later we could see the same attitude emerging towards his fiancée, his parents and his friends. No one was felt to be able actually to help him: on one occasion he very nearly spoiled an important meeting he had set up on prisoners' rights because he had refused to delegate any responsibility for it to anyone else. It often appeared that the prisoners were representative of his objects who he kept imprisoned inside himself, having to be repetitively 'helped' because he couldn't allow them to be free from his control of them.

The patient held several beliefs about me which were clung to with an unquestioning conviction and were never subject to examination. One, which I mentioned earlier, was that I came from the same city in the United States that he did. Another was that he was my only male patient. He had commented on this several times – he had never seen a man leaving the consulting room before his session nor arriving as he left and therefore he took as absolute fact that he was the only male. One day, in the third year of his analysis, he saw a man coming from the area of my consulting room before his session; this repeated itself the same day over the following couple of weeks. At first, he commented that it was funny to see a man in the building at that time, he wondered where he thought he was going. After a couple of weeks he said it occurred to him that perhaps the man was a student, coming to me for supervision. I took this up quite gently at first, but eventually commented that he was avoiding another possible explanation – the possibility that this man was my patient – that this avoidance was unquestioned and unquestionable, and that I thought that was the most remarkable thing about it.

The patient was silent for a minute or two, and when he spoke his voice was full of barely controlled rage. How dare I tell him about my other patients? This is none of his business, nothing to do with him, I am trying to 'get' him, to humiliate him ... and show him how much more I know than he does; he has obviously touched some very sore spot of my own and for some reason I am on the attack, giving him information he is not interested in and doesn't want to know.

It is difficult to convey the violence of his response; I was shocked by it. In the few minutes left in the session I attempted to explore what he was feeling, while feeling quite shaken myself. He came to the following session in a state of great agitation; he could no longer trust me, he felt everything about the analysis and my capacity to treat him was in question, and he was not sure the analysis ought to continue.

Over the following days, and indeed weeks and months, we worked with this experience. There are of course many aspects to it which we explored and which are worth discussing. But what I would like to focus on are not the particular constituents of the particular phantasy that was interfered with (he is the only male) – I would like to emphasize the catastrophic effect of discovering that I am not exactly as he has created me – or that things are not exactly as he would have them be. I think that what the patient was confronted with at the moment I gently queried his conviction was the sudden possibility that I am not a product of his mind; that there is a difference between his phantasy of who I am, and who I actually may be.

The event itself was recovered from; the analysis continued. But it had alerted me, and I think the patient himself, to the omnipotence of his phantasies, and to how they could operate quite casually, unexamined, alongside what he felt was a good working relationship. I began to be more tuned into the ubiquitous nature of the idealizing transference, and the contempt and condescension which lay underneath.

The contempt and triumph behind all this almost never showed itself directly; one had to be on the alert for it, because the patient himself felt consciously appreciative and cooperative. What I felt was a vague sense of unease that things sometimes seemed to be going a little too smoothly, and, at the same time, and paradoxically, a real fear that I couldn't understand about confronting the patient in a more forceful, less pussy-footing way about what I was beginning to understand about the pervasiveness of his manic-defensive structure.

This became clearer when I interpreted on a Monday that the horrible feelings he described himself having had over the weekend were to do with an experience of being stuck alone with terrible feelings, trapped with them, and now missing analysis painfully. On Tuesday he reported that he felt better, and thought this was to do with my interpretation about the weekend – it made sense of what he'd felt on the weekend. He added that on the Friday, when I'd spoken about the weekend to come, in preparation, as it were, he had had the thought, 'She has to say that; it's part of the ritual; that's what "they" [analysts] say.'

We could speak, then, about the ways this quiet, chronic mocking denigration goes on all the time: how he often listens with 'half-an ear' to what I say, takes it with a grain of salt, assuming (not quite unconsciously) that I don't really mean it, or think it either. We began to understand the way these 'assumptions' about things which were unspoken, but felt to be somehow 'understood' between us, served insidiously to undermine the real work of the analysis.

What I feel happens in the patient's rage is that he is suddenly confronted by the difference between the reality he has constructed, and the reality he is confronted with. This is unbearable because if he is him and I am me, then he has to look at the sham world he has created.

In summary, we began to see what he can and does do to his objects:

1   What I have called chronic mild contempt, exemplified in the under-
    lying unexamined conviction that I don't really mean what I say, that I
    am going through the motions for some spurious reasons of my own,
    and that he doesn't have to actually listen to what I say or to take it
    seriously. (This phenomenon seems to me to be similar to Bion's obser-
    vation that, for members of a group he was leading, 'an unshakable
    belief that they are justified in thinking I am qualified by training and
    experience to lead the group, is matched by an almost equally unshak-
    able indifference to everything I say'; Bion, 1961, p. 83) In this sense
    many assumed-to-be-shared concepts in the analysis are only experi-
    enced between inverted commas: 'missing the analysis', 'the weekend',
    'your other patients' can all be talked about, but there is an assumption
    that we both know they don't really have any meaning. The point about
    this that I want to stress is the contempt and condescension the patient
    feels towards the analyst, who is also felt to be pretending. (Of course,
    this can be greatly exacerbated by situations where the analyst has, for
    one reason or another, lost her sense of real conviction about what she
    is interpreting. If the analyst is 'going through the motions' when she is
    interpreting to her patient, the patient's sense that the analyst is also a
    sham, that, indeed, there are only sham, false, objects, with whom one
    can only have pretend trustworthy relationships, is confirmed.) One
    aspect of this pretence can be a secret belief in the patient that he, the
    patient, is really an analyst 'in all but name' (e.g. minus a few qualifica-
    tions) and that the analyst is really an analyst 'in name only'.
2   He can and does attack his internal object in the same way he attacked
    his fiancée – in which it/I can become suddenly completely worthless –
    an experience he believes in absolutely. Another way of putting this is
    that he experiences the loss of his good internal object: attacking it, he
    loses his love for it, and therefore he loses it inside himself. He has to
    cover that up, to mask his feelings of desperation about his incapacity to
    care for and protect his love for his objects inside himself. The ego is
    kept alive by the love of the internal object; the internal object is only
    kept alive by the ego's love for it. It is not kept alive by spurious
    admiration or idealization. Contrary to what the patient seems to
    believe, idealization is not love with a little bit of extra enthusiasm
    tagged on. Idealization is the opposite of love.
3   Indeed, part of the patient's contempt consists in an unexamined belief
    that his objects are actually of no use to him; while he and they go
    through the motion of pretending they are playing their part, and are the
    'support' he maintains he thinks they are. This became increasingly
    obvious in the analysis as we were able to look at the curious 'double-
    think' he was able to do: on the one hand, feeling dependent and
    grateful, but on the other hand, and simultaneously, being secretly

dismissive, not actually believing the analyst could take the full weight of him, for instance could bear to know about his real contempt, or real vicious attacks. (This capacity for doublethink deserves more attention than I can give to it here. It bears some resemblance to what Ruth Malcolm (1990) describes as the 'slicing' of experience, and is similar to what John Steiner (1985) has called 'turning a blind eye'. It seems to me most to resemble Bion's description of 'reversible perspective' but where each of the two mutually contradictory points of view is held by the patient at the same time. This seems to require a hair-thin, but profound split in the ego.) In the same way, the patient's friends, colleagues and even his fiancée were not really trusted to help him: he once spoke about being given an 'honorary' position somewhere, and I often thought most of the figures in his life were established in a kind of 'honorary' position – he had 'honorary' friends, and an 'honorary' analyst, but nobody who was allowed or expected to actually get down and do the job.

Opposed to all this contempt and condescension is the tiny bit of hope that his capacity to care for and love his objects may not be entirely dead, that something genuinely loving may still be alive in him. But this is a fragile hope, and it is constantly being weakened by his myriad little undermining movements.

Our work in this area was greatly helped by two dreams he had, within some few months of each other. In the first:

> He is at the Grand Canyon (a place where he has never been but has longed to go to) and is overwhelmed by its beauty. The feeling in the dream was of extreme happiness at the realization that it really was even more beautiful, more awesome, than he had expected or imagined it. And then suddenly he realized that actually it was Disneyland, and that the whole thing was a trick, a sleight of hand.

I thought the dream, which could be felt to be about his idealization, was actually about his perception of his real love for his object. The Grand Canyon was more than he could have imagined it to be. I thought it becomes Disneyland in the dream both because it has to be something constructible, creatable by a Disney-himself, who can create mock-ups of what is real, but also because it then feels false and just a mock-up, a sleight of hand because of his contempt and mockery of it. The dream conveys a beginning realization that what he does to his objects destroys their good-ness- makes them false in his mind.

In the second dream:

> He is taking a train trip across the United States in an Amtrak 'bubble-top' train with his parents. He explains that these are trains which make the trans-continental trip with large, all-glass observation cars – he had

done this as a boy with his parents. In the dream he was sitting in the top of one of these cars, as though it was a double-decker bus. Suddenly his mother was not there ... he was aware that she wasn't there ... and he went down the stairs to find her. At the bottom of the train the car was filled with mud – like a swamp – and he saw a woman's body, small, and looking horribly deformed, and covered in mud.

He said it was a horrible dream. He found himself not wanting to tell me about it. He thought the woman in the dream, who was not actually his mother, probably also was his mother. And the train reminded him of the trains to the concentration camps, though of course nothing could be more different, he said, than these beautiful bubble top trains from those closed filthy, freezing cars of the trains to the death camps.

The dream gave us a vivid look at what goes on inside him: on top, he sits up high with the parents – crossing the entire country, getting its measure. Underneath that is the horror of where he actually keeps me, and his parents, in his mind – in the smelly, muddy bottom part of his mind, where I am belittled and deformed.

The two dreams – one coming several weeks after the other – present a striking picture of the patient's movement during an important period in the analysis. The first dream describes an immediate and surprising apprehension of his love for (and awe of) the hugeness of his object: it (she) is more grand – bigger, grander – and more 'beautiful' in his mind than he had allowed. I think this is a startling recognition of his apprehension of the enormity, the hugeness of his good object in his mind – when he can see it. But in this dream the bubble of the idealization – the mania – turns the experience into a sham: it is just Disneyland ... a make-believe has-to-be-Grand-Canyon ... the exaggeration is an attempt to keep the object Grand, but of course it destroys its reality, and its actual goodness.

The second dream, coming several weeks later, has an entirely different tone. In the beginning the patient/dreamer is in a 'bubble-top' car, viewing the whole length of the country from up high, above everyone else. But the dream then remorselessly focuses on the rest of the scene: his mother suddenly isn't there, he is looking for her but cannot find her ... he goes downstairs and finds the ground covered in mud and a small, deformed body ... and he is reminded of the trains to the concentration camps. He himself remarks that there cannot be any greater difference than that between those high up bubble topped trains occupied by privileged little boys with their families, and the trains to the death camps.

This is a dream which comes from another position. I think at this moment my patient is at the threshold of the depressive position. The manic idealization is still there, powerfully, in the beginning of the sequence: he is in the high up place he always wanted to be in, has a view of the whole landscape from where he sits. But the dream leads to another, disturbing sight – to the object remorselessly left in the mud down at the bottom of his mind.

At the moment he can have this dream, he is aware both of his love for his objects and his often disastrous treatment of them. This is enormously painful.

As working through the dreams brought all this home to him, the patient experienced feelings which were new to him: at first, a different kind of sad depression which he was frightened of. At the same time as these feelings of trepidation, he began to feel a sense of some relief and some renewed optimism about himself. He felt solider.

Conclusion

In this chapter I have explored some of the dynamics behind the experience of losing one's feelings of being able to love, and thus losing one's belief in being loved by one's objects. I have particularly tried to show the relationship between idealization and contempt, and how they work together to prevent an establishment of internal security.

In fact, as mature adults we lose and recover our love for our objects all the time: we are jealous and envious, intolerant and possessive, greedy and triumphant towards them. And then, at our best, we recognize our attacks on our objects, recover our love for them, and restore them to their own identity within us. It is in our nature to be ambivalent towards our objects; we cannot change that. What we can do is to know about our ambivalence. This is not a blissful state of being, but it is lively and permits us to continue to grow in relation to our self and our objects.

The 'sham' state of mind, which is supported by idealization, doesn't allow for this ebb and flow of a real relationship – doesn't allow for the loss and recovery of love. It reduces the unique specificity of a particular person to undifferentiated sameness – the sameness of the idealization, and the sameness of the contempt which accompanies it.

A person's psychic structure can be described in terms of his relationship to his internal objects, that is, in terms of the ways in which he has managed to establish good objects inside himself, and how he copes with and organizes the threats to their well-being. This is, of course, what we know as the working through of the depressive position. It is a continuous, life-long process, and is what allows for the richness of internal life and development of relationships.

References

Bion, W. (1961) *Experiences in Groups*. New York: Basic Books.

Deutsch, H. (1933) The Psychology of Manic-Depressive States, with Particular Reference to Clinical Hypomania. In H. Deutsch, *Neuroses and Character Types*. New York: International University Press [1965].

Freud, S. (1909). Notes upon a Case of Obsessional Neurosis. In J. Strachey (ed.), *The Standard Edition of the Complete Psychological Works of Sigmund Freud*, vol. 10. London: Hogarth Press [1955].

Freud, S. (1917) Mourning and Melancholia. In J. Strachey (ed.), *The Standard Edition of the Complete Psychological Works of Sigmund Freud*, vol. 14. London: Hogarth Press [1957].

Freud, S. (1911) Formulations on the Two Principles of Mental Functioning. In J. Strachey (ed.), *The Standard Edition of the Complete Psychological Works of Sigmund Freud*, vol. 12. London: Hogarth Press [1958].

Freud, S. (1923) The Ego and The Id. In J. Strachey (ed.), *The Standard Edition of the Complete Psychological Works of Sigmund Freud*, vol. 19. London: Hogarth Press [1961].

Klein, M. (1935) A Contribution to the Psycho-genesis of Manic-Depressive States. In M. Klein, *Contributions to Psycho-Analysis* (pp. 282–310). London: Hogarth Press [1965].

Malcolm, R. (1990) As If: The Phenomenon of Not Learning. *International Journal of Psycho-analysis* 71: 385–391.

Riviere, J. (1936) A Contribution to the Analysis of the Negative Therapeutic Reaction. *International Journal of Psychoanalysis* 17: 304–320.

Segal, H. (1981) *The Work of Hanna Segal: A Kleinian Approach to Clinical Practice*. New York: Jason Aronson.

Steiner, J. (1985) Turning a Blind Eye: The Cover-up for Oedipus. *International Review of Psycho-Analysis* 12: 161–172.

5 'I Used to Think You Were Wonderful'

The Persecution/Idealization Cycle of Melancholia

Priscilla Roth

In this chapter I discuss how a patient strove to protect herself from the pain of object loss by rearranging her perception of reality – and often my own – in order to maintain her internal attachment to a pathological object relationship. This relationship was characterized by the idealization of the object, believed to be almost available but cruelly withheld, and, simultaneously, rage at this object for its refusal to be what she needed it to be. By contrast, I was required, over and over again, painfully to experience the loss which the patient herself largely managed to avoid.

I describe some of the shifts that occurred in the sessions, reflecting the patient's slowly increasing capacity to face pain and the awareness of loss.

Idealization and Persecution

Idealization is described by Melanie Klein in two different ways. When she writes that 'The whole of [the infant's] instinctual desires and his unconscious phantasies imbue the breast with qualities going far beyond the actual nourishment it affords' and repeatedly stresses that the mother's introjected loved and loving good breast forms 'the core of the [infant's] ego' (Klein, 1957, p. 180), Klein is suggesting that the original good object must be experienced as ideal – nothing less than this would adequately convey 'the whole of (the infant's) instinctual desires'. In this view, the infant projects his entire loving capacity onto the object, and this projected-into object is then introjected, together with its actual goodness, to become his very core (Likierman, 2001, p. 95).

At other moments, though, idealization is viewed differently, for Klein also frequently maintained that much of what the infant experiences as positive is in fact the result of a defensive exaggeration of the object's goodness: 'Idealization is bound up with the splitting of the object, for the good aspects of the breast are exaggerated as a safeguard against the fear of the persecuting breast'; that is, a defence against persecutory anxieties stemming from the infant's projection of hateful impulses and hate-filled parts of the self into the (bad) breast/mother (Klein, 1946, p. 7).

DOI: 10.4324/9781003588870-7

These two views are not, I think, contradictory: it was Klein's view that at the beginning of life splitting must be sufficiently impermeable to ensure the normal necessary separation of good from bad. In this view, idealization was not simply a psychopathological mechanism, but an essential intermediate 'process in the young child's mind, since he cannot yet cope with his fears of persecution'. Not until a second stage, that is, 'not until early anxieties have been sufficiently relieved owing to experiences which increase love and trust, is it possible to establish the all-important process of bringing together the various aspects of objects' (Klein, 1940, p. 315, footnote). Thus, 'the neonate can cope with life only by actively separating out the forces of destruction from those energies considered constructive ... the forces tending toward life, object love and integration of the ego must be united into a coherent whole before the unity of the real object in its good and bad aspects can be faced' (Petot, 1991, p. 211).

It is thus only in a second phase – as ego capacities develop and depressive possibilities thereby arise – that splitting must become more porous – allowing confrontations – temporary at first – between love and hate. But it is worth noting that in her last paper, Klein returned to the problem of idealization, remarking that 'In my experience, the need for idealization is never fully given up, even though in normal development the facing of internal and external reality tends to diminish it' (Klein, 1963, p. 305).

Since the most pernicious factor in developmental disturbances is the blurring of primary splitting between good and bad: that is, envy, it follows that a defence against envy would have to include undiminished impermeable idealization.

Envy is born of the gap between the expectation accompanying the fantasy of an inexhaustible breast, and reality, which inevitably brings deprivation. This 'inexhaustible' breast is conceived as giving perfect satisfaction to a perfect self. Essential to this phantasy is no differentiation whatsoever between perfect self/perfect breast: a unified and undifferentiated couple. When it exists – however briefly – it is subjectively the totality of experience. The idealness of the ideal breast is not only that it nourishes and loves: the ideal breast creates an ideal self – an entirely loving self from whom all feelings of badness – of hatred, rage, persecution – have been expunged.

The bad, that is, persecuting, breast is not the self. Because it contains, by projection, the split off destructive impulses and parts of the self, it is conceived as cruelly and malevolently withholding satisfaction, thereby projecting bad feelings: hatred and envy – into the self. For the small infant, this too, when it exists, is the whole world, now intolerable, and these experiences have to be got rid of and are re-projected into the bad breast which becomes both more terrifying and more vengefully re-projecting badness: anxiety/hatred/terror/rage back into the self.

What I intend to show in the material that follows are, first, the contours and the strength of my patient's dependence on the melancholic solution to manage overwhelming anxieties presented by the intrusion of reality into her omnipotent phantasies. Her 'solution' involved the maintenance of a powerful split in her object, allowing the possibility of a perfect ideal object with whom she is inseparably bound in pure love; irrevocably kept distinct from a terrifying hateful persecuting object. This of course is a configuration we all know well. What I will then explore is the movement/transformation of this impermeable split into another, no less destructive, form when the analysis, and ordinary life, confront the patient with the beginnings of an awareness of reality.

While idealization is used by K to protect her from powerful experiences of envy of her good object, in fact it imprisons her in a world of dissatisfaction, disappointment and self hatred and indeed, proliferating experiences of envy and jealousy of other people who come to stand for the idealized primal object.

Clinical Material

In her early thirties, when her analysis began, K had had several boyfriends, but none of the relationships had lasted. She was puzzled about this; afraid she would never get married and have children, never be 'normal'.

She is a lawyer in an established firm; she was beautiful, accomplished, from a wealthy family. She reports that she had constant temper tantrums as a child and was felt to be impossible to control. She has two younger sisters.

For the first year K expressed only positive feelings about the analysis, often remarking on how much 'progress' she was making. She had had a previous unsuccessful analysis, and she saw this new analysis as full of promise. From the beginning her material was strikingly narcissistic – a running commentary on her feelings, in a vacuum, with almost no content. After the first year there was a change, as she became angry about breaks or occasional alterations to the structure of the analysis; the rare changed session time infuriated her, as did any variation in what she saw as usual analytic practice: 'No one else's analyst takes off the week *before* Easter; everyone else's analyst takes the week *after* Easter.'

Looking back now, what becomes clear was a hopeful beginning, where it was possible that I would fit perfectly into her expectations and hopes of me. And then: disappointment.

During the first two years K went on occasional dates and had some sexual relationships; none of these had any importance to her. In the third year she had a date with a young man, B, which became a 'wonderful' weekend spent together. She was delighted with him and soon reported that she was in love. However, within weeks, these feelings of attraction transformed into complaints, demands and assertions of entitlement. By the third week after the exciting 'wonderful' weekend, the patient was irritated with B for not being sufficiently committed: she nagged him with increasing bitterness about smoking, untidiness, not having a driving licence, not answering her text messages quickly enough, not going around the car and opening the car door for her like her friend's boyfriend did, and not taking her on romantic holidays. He was her possession, expected to provide her with all the accoutrements of a 'relationship'. From this point on, I never heard about the pleasures of getting to know B, delight in his company, or anything specific to him that might interest or please her. He was consistently described in terms of what her idea of 'a boyfriend' or 'a relationship' should be. When he occasionally rebelled and became angry, she would arrive at her session in despair about having gone too far, wanting help to control her behaviour. This never lasted long; within minutes she would find reasons to justify her attack on him and to find further fault with him.

It was not difficult to recognize this as a repetition of the analytic relationship, and of course both as repetitions of a fundamental primitive relationship. I also think that she consistently only brought to the analysis the negative aspects of her marriage, almost always being out of touch, during the sessions, with its good aspects, both because of the real, unconscious need to 'cure' the primitive relationship, but also because her 'complaining' was the most compelling and vivid way in which she could unconsciously communicate to her analyst the experience of the transference.

Two Sessions

One day I spoke to K about a fee raise. The following day she responded:

> I really don't want to come to analysis anymore. Don't want four times a week. I'd rather sleep. I want to come once a week. I want to be able to come if I feel bad … but not all the time. I used to feel bad, needed to come more. Now I don't. I came to analysis because I wanted to have a relationship – well, now I've got one, I just want to live my life. Not have to analyse myself all the time. Like normal people.

The proposed fee raise had insulted her and hurt her feelings. The very fact of the fee – and the raising of it – stood for everything that keeps her out and differentiates her role from mine, her position from mine. She experiences this as an expulsion. Threatened with the loss to her sense of herself and to the reality she has created, she instead incorporated a particular picture of me into herself and, as it were, became this view of me: she identified with a cold and unavailable version of me and became herself cold and unavailable, someone with no needs and who herself contains everything desirable. At the same time she projected all her sense of inadequacy and worthlessness into me. Once in the grip of this two-way projective identification, why would she want to come to useless me for analysis? The threat of object-loss is avoided by an identification with the loved and hated object: the patient pulling her analyst into an enactment of her primary libidinal relationship. In this situation: *I raise her fee/she feels contemptible* becomes she *is cold and smug/I am contemptible*. The relationship: subject to object – child to parent – remains the same; one person is a useless supplicant, the other a cold and impenetrable figure. Relations between the two are exploitative and ruthless one way or the other, but the basic relationship stays the same.

Melancholia is a narcissistic condition; at base, the hatred of the object in melancholia is because of its separateness from the self, but this situation is complicated by other feelings. The wished-for perfect object is inseparable from the perfect self and the perfect self is entirely loving and therefore lovable. Made of love. The horrible thing I do by raising K's fee is make her feel hate-full and therefore hateful (to me) and therefore the object of wilful persecution from me.

That night the patient had a dream that she brought to the next day's session:

> *I was coming here, to my session. Maybe it was summer, because it was warm and sunny. All around the building was water, there was a big lake and a beautiful garden – a beautiful landscape. To get to the door I had to climb onto a ladder, and there was a pulley system which pulled me in, over the lake, as if over a moat. At the door, three girls came out – they'd been in the consulting room with you. They said 'She's marking one of your essays – she's got some of your work on her table.' I realized that they were just supervisees, and they thought I was just a supervisee; they didn't realize I'm in analysis. When I went in you said 'K', very warmly and friendly and nice, and you showed me pictures of plans for the gardens. As if we were friends.*

This dream – a response to the proposed fee raise – is the other side of the melancholia. In the dream, K recovers the ideal place from which she is now not excluded. If the fee raise was felt to put her down, in *this* place I reach out and 'pully' her up, like a small infant, and bring her to me. And I have her on my table – in my mind – all the time. Not coming (and of course having to go) every day – but in my mind all the time. A never-ending session in which I show her beautiful gardens and we are friends forever. This is the idealized relationship, felt to be lost the previous day and magically restored in her dream. In this place she is entirely loved and loveable and loving, as am I. We are 'friends'.

The dream reality is so clearly about 'Up' and 'Down'. The fee raise threw her down; the dream image is concretely about being pulled back up. 'Up' is not only being together, parallel, with me, but is 'Upper' than the 'just supervisees' who are looked down on. When she is up with me, I am warm and she is warm – the hatred of the previous day is completely non-existent – as if it never was. When she is up with me she can feel love-full. Not hate-full.

A few months later, after a summer break, K announced that things had been terrible the whole time 'we were away'. She was horrible to B, critical and nasty, feeling that he wasn't good enough.

Yesterday, she said, they nearly got to the end. Saturday her sister gave birth:

> We went to see them in the hospital yesterday. B and I were both born in that same hospital. On the way in, I said to B, 'Isn't it amazing that we were born here too?' He said, 'Yeah'; he was not very interested. I just went nuts! And then, there they were: my sister and brother-in-law, there with their baby. My younger sister now has two children! And I was furious! I hated B, I told him he isn't what I want, he isn't good enough.

I said I thought the experience of visiting the new baby was both upsetting to her in itself, but also powerfully representative of a frequent experience she has; I said there is always a picture in the back of her mind of where she'd really like to be and can't be. It is *where she is not*. Mother and father and baby together – with her having to look on, completely left out – is the awful apotheosis of it. After a moment I said I thought that in the background is the picture she'd had of me on holiday, when things had been, as she said, 'terrible' for her: me 'not interested' in her and not remembering that she was born here too – that she has a place here in my mind too. When she feels so forgotten, so jealous, then B – who can't or won't make everything perfectly better – seems to her not good enough, however he behaves.

I felt sympathetic and tender towards her.

K immediately said she didn't understand. The baby visits only happened yesterday, and she was horrible all through the holiday.

I explained again that this was only the culmination ... that the whole holiday 'when we were away' felt like having to watch a happy family – from which she was excluded – in her mind. I mentioned also her parents and baby sister – that watching this new baby brought back these memories and ever-threatening feelings.

(I felt uncomfortable explaining this again; I thought that her not understanding was disingenuous: I felt thrown.)

She responded, 'But how can I have felt that about two parents who were always fighting with each other?' (I again felt she was being disingenuous – a kind of mock stupidity.)

After a few minutes she said, quietly, 'I *was* jealous of L [her friend] this weekend ... I was mad with jealousy.' L's new boyfriend had 'whisked L away to Prague on a holiday to a glamorous hotel. He planned it all!' K had said to B, 'You never do this!' She was overcome with jealousy – thought she wouldn't be able to bear it, wouldn't be able to live. There was a long pause. Then she said: during the holiday she didn't love B at all. Didn't even respect him. She had to go through the motions. (This was said with sadness.) She paused. And then: 'So what does what you've been saying have to do with *that*? I mean, why didn't I feel any respect for him?'

This is a complicated message, and I want to look at it carefully:

On the one hand, I believe that for a moment there actually had been a shift in K's thinking: she had taken in what I'd said about jealousy and could tell me that she is able to be aware of jealousy and how powerful it is – so powerful that, drowning in her jealous and I think envious feelings, she was unable to love B during the holiday. For a moment she is sad about this. But as soon as she experiences a wish that I help her to understand it, two things happen: she immediately feels envious of the privileged position this wish of hers gives *me*: as if I am now the lucky one, like L, who is being 'whisked off' – and up – now by her – to a glamorous, enviable place. 'So, what does what you've been saying have to do with *that*?' – and I am suddenly dropped again and have no link to her and am in a contemptible position.

At the same time, I am being told about someone – her – who doesn't respect someone – B, me – and has to 'go through the motions'. If this second scenario is what is going on here, now – if she is contemptuous of my concern for her and condescendingly placating a me who has been trying to get through to her – what does it suggest about the first scenario?

It is my belief that both are true. I think that K is actually able to remember and communicate to me something about her own jealousy and envy. And then the envy provoked from this movement towards a me experienced as helpful and at the same time not-her – attacks and corrupts a meaningful communication. '*So, what does what you've been saying have to do with that?*' is an envious attack on her sudden picture of me who has been 'whisked off' to an enviable place in her mind. But the attack is more destructive than that: it is also a distortion of her own sense of the ordinary helpfulness of her analyst; from one second to the next, she is 'going through the motions'.

Being on the receiving end of this is a temporarily difficult experience: feeling dropped, confused, wrong-footed.

But for K, something much more substantial has taken place: a moment's communication, a moment's sadness about herself and what she can do, what she is like. And then the recognition and understanding are not only destroyed, they are corrupted. K's nature, and the nature of her psychopathology, forces her into a hate-full state of mind, produced by envy of the even momentarily satisfying object. Directed at her good, and therefore hated object.

Being full of hatred is a horrible state of mind.

As a defence against this awareness of a self full of hatred, and therefore hateful, and therefore hated, K needs to create or cling to those few moments when she somehow, as if magically, felt completely loving. She knows this perfect place exists because she once had it: that first 'wonderful' weekend with B before it all went wrong, the idyllic landscape dream; these remain perfect and always possible and attainable in her mind. This perfect state is all that saves her from the suffering created by this impossible state of mind.

K can only be alright if she is together, absolutely, with her object: the object as a 'we' with her. In this sense 'We were born here too' doesn't only mean 'we were both born in this hospital – the hospital where my sister's baby was just born'. It means 'you and I were born at exactly the same moment, came into existence as a "we". There was no you before me.' B's uninterested 'yeah' dropped her from a 'we' to a hateful 'me'. Similarly, I must only begin my existence as she opened her eyes to me. My crime is that being myself – remaining her analyst – I don't protect her from an increasing awareness that I am not born here in this room as she notices me.

I think it is likely that 'normal' for K means everyone else in the world, imagined as existing in perpetual unity with an object. I also think that, para-doxically, K's envy for everyone else is envy that they can be an 'I' without desperation or devastating envy, and without possession of an object.

Appreciating the goodness of the object makes her instantly vulnerable to terrible persecution. The split *idealized object/bad object* having to be so rigidly maintained means that the bad object – who contains her bad, murderous, hateful projections, and her bad, murderous hateful self – will, by its very ima-gined nature, attack her with all the rage and envy she has projected into it. Furthermore, if I *am* felt to have been able – even for a moment – to withstand and contain her projections, she is besieged by envy of my ability for some actual goodness, momentarily recognized by her. This is the problem: the object has to be perfect – and then can never be real or actualized – because its actual good qualities are always under terrible immediate attack.

Sometime Later, Two Weeks before a Three-Week Break

The patient has four sessions a week – Monday through Thursday. She had, unusually, cancelled two Monday mornings in a row.

When she returned on Tuesday, she reported that she'd had a miserable weekend, and that she now felt depressed, mean and ungenerous. She reported a dream. In this dream, *she and B take her sister's two small chil-dren into their bed. They were all in bed together; it was very very nice.*

She added that on her way to analysis she always sees women in big cars, with children. Why can't she be happy like them? They always look so happy. She is fed up with B, wondering if she'd be happier on her own.

I thought – and said to her – that the dream was like her dream about coming to the consulting room in the idyllic landscape. Here it is about grownups and children all in her bed, all very happy. Like the idyllic land-scape dream, this is a dream about something she feels she should have, did once have, and, compared with which everything else is tormentingly dis-appointing. This in bed with children dream is also a dream-solution to the hospital experience where she had visited her sister and brother-in-law after the birth of their second child. In this new dream, not only does she, together with B, replace the sister and brother-in-law, standing for the parents with their new baby, her sister, but she and B are also the children she has taken into her bed. All jealousy, all envy, all sense of being left and alone is obviated by this dream.

But it is also worth noting that the phrase 'in bed together' suggests 'in collusion with'. In this sense I think this is not simply a daydreamy dream of a wished-for event sometime in the future. As itself it is an envious take-over of everything in the primal scene: stealing and thus attacking every position, every identity, every experience.

I suspect that K knows that something gets spoilt by the omnipotent dream/ phantasy. And perhaps that she continues to maintain a corrupt position in her analysis in collusion with an analyst who either is blind to her corruption or in collusion with it for her own reasons.

One of these reasons is felt to be my own narcissism – a view of her object who, in possession of good things, doesn't give them to her, (is not ever-bountiful, ever generous) but who, instead keeps them for herself. The women with the big cars, the mother with the full breast – kept for her own smug self-satisfied self.

When she returned the following week, she was very angry: 'What you said Thursday really irritated me. I slept badly again. You said I was feeling fragmented because I missed the sessions last Monday and this. A stupid thing to say.'

This was not what I had said, and I thought she knew this. I felt in a familiar uncomfortable spot.

I said, 'It sounds like this has become something I have said in your mind, though it's not what I said.'

She said:

> I know ... you said it's because you are taking the holiday as well. That makes me even more irritated. You're saying that I sleep badly, that I feel bad, because of something you do. *You always take things up in terms of here.* Maybe you think it's your job. It's just stupid. And the answer is obviously to stop coming; if analysis is my problem, why bother coming? I can solve my problems by not coming.

What 'irritates' K is my insistence that there is an 'I' – separate from her – *who matters to her.* To have to be aware of my – felt to be incorrigibly narcissistic – insistence on my importance to her is intolerable. We are not a 'we' – I am a 'me' and I am insisting that something I do matters to her. She can only deal with this by annihilating me: not coming.

> You should think about the impact on me when you say these things. I leave on Thursday, you tell me it's my fault for missing last Monday and this Monday. Your job is to make me feel better. *And if what you say is true*, how come I slept fine on Thursday and Friday, then terribly on Saturday, Sunday, and Monday? How does that make sense? I don't find what you say interesting ... I'm not interested in analysis.

Here she is absolutely clear: my job is to make her feel better. To take away all her bad feelings, including her resentment and hatred of me. But a moment later there is a very slight movement … 'and if what you say is true' – the possibility of being able for a second to consider. And then 'How does that make sense. I'm not interested in analysis'. The door between us, open for a second, is snapped shut.

I think this is a powerful and immediate projection of an experience of K's when the implacably maintained delusion of unity between self and object is pulled from her: when she is suddenly dropped; repeating what I picture as an infantile experience: that the nipple – believed to be her possession – is suddenly pulled from her mouth.

Aware of the brief opening, I reminded her of previous weeks, when I thought she had been interested, and I said something had happened to her interest.

There was a pause and then she said, 'I haven't felt that in a long time.' She paused again. 'I used to think you were wonderful. You understood me *perfectly* … all I ever wanted.' And then: 'How do you explain *that*!?'

Again, just for a moment, K was thoughtful: remembering, considering, describing. And talking to me from a place where we were at the same time separate from each other and able to helpfully communicate something. But the last statement – 'How do you explain *that*?', taunting and triumphant – shuts the door in my face.

After a few minutes I tried to talk to her about some of this. I said my impression is as if at these moments I'm kept on a very thin ledge, that I can't make any contact with her – can't get in, can't feel any real understanding between us … that she swats me away so that I can't touch her. We're allowed only the shortest moment of contact, and then her mind closes suddenly, as if she doesn't want understanding either way between us – for me to understand her, or for her to understand me.

She was silent and then said, 'That's like my father. What he does. There is no contact, he doesn't allow it. This is just what it feels like to be with him. He talks only in clichés. And my mother … only neediness.' She paused.

> My father is moving house – after 30 years – the house I grew up in has been torn to the ground – they're building a new house on the property. The house is gone. It's very odd. He says it is a difficult time for him, but he only talks in clichés. 'It's a very emotional time for me.' Meaningless.

She was again silent for a minute. In fact, she said, she's in quite a good mood today. Not here – she's been in a bad mood since she got here – but she woke up in a good mood even though she didn't get much sleep. On the weekend they moved B's stuff into her flat – the vans came and delivered everything. On Saturday they put his stuff away. It was fun. There is still lots of crap around … boxes and things. But they did a lot. On Sunday they went to a wedding – then came back last night … She's excited about the coming holiday, but not about the flights: there will be a long flight, then two internal short flights … she is afraid of the short flights.

I said I thought that what I had said had made sense to her, and that as well as talking about her trip, she was describing a change that seems to have taken place now, in which her mind can actually move and travel. I thought this was very different from where she had been earlier in the session: that her thoughts seemed now to be able to move out of the flatness and thin-ness, the batting back. She now had thoughts about her father and mother, about moving house, and putting stuff away, about travelling, and how it will all be ... Her mind and thoughts seemed freer, with more possibilities. I thought she had been able to make room for me in her mind, as she is able to make room for B in her flat.

She paused and then said, 'I am meeting the woman from human resources today at work. She is a psychotherapist. She is apparently very odd. E says this woman will offer me supervision. That'll be weird.' She spoke again about the trips and that she wished she could stay in one place.

I said I thought that she was finding it 'very odd' that something had happened inside her, that she felt freer and less constricted, without her being in charge of it, being able to predict it or explain it. I thought she didn't know how to think about that and found it 'weird', but I thought that she felt it had something to do with my human resources.

The session ended.

The following day she announced that she was furious at B. She had come home from work and found that he hadn't moved any of the boxes she'd asked him to get rid of.

'He doesn't do anything for *us*', she shouted. 'He will do all sorts of things for himself, he tidies up *his* room, but he left boxes all around the house ... he never thinks about *us*. Either he should earn the money, and drive me around in his car, or else he has to help me clean up the flat. He has to do one or other. He has to be a partner.'

What has happened? For some minutes in the previous day's session – longer than usual – K had been able to be more available, more open, her mind moving and connecting and flexible; freer to follow her thoughts and wanting to communicate them. This is, for these minutes, an emergence from a narcissistic state into a real relationship with another person *and it is an accomplishment*. But as she experiences ordinary helpful contact with another person, she is aware that it is 'weird' and 'odd'. Me being me – with my ordinary *human resources* – talking to her, telling her something that interests her, is disturbing and dangerous because almost immediately it provokes envy.

And then the session ended. I ended the session; I am suddenly up, she is down. I am 'supervising' her.

At that point she needs to revert to her narcissistic defences as powerfully as ever, and this includes the projection of narcissism into me: 'He [*she*] doesn't do anything for *us*. He [*she*] will do all sort of things for himself – tidying up his [*her*] room ...' These are hate-full feelings, by which I mean both full of hatred and also felt to be hateful – bad. Not 'normal'. When I don't protect her from them, when I just take care of *me*, I am not tidying up her mental room – her mind. I am leaving her with the horrible mess while I drive around in my big car.

It is at the moment of separateness that the good object becomes cruel: keeping her resources for herself, looking down on the patient who suddenly doesn't have any. For as soon as we are not as-one, every good interpretation is a bad interpretation: I have become superior and narcissistic. And the ordinary goodness of the object creates unmanageable envy. No longer an absolute split, this state is much worse than persecution by the persecuting object: this state provokes constant attacking, constant undermining.

For K, there *are* moments of 'wonderful': a first weekend and maybe two short weeks with B, when she could actually love him. An idyllic landscape dream of being in my mind and heart forever. An imagined scene in which she is the parents and she is the children and – since she has created this and occupies every position in it – there is only love: no hatred, no jealousy, no envy. And of course, the first weeks of her analysis when she thought I was wonderful – I understood her 'perfectly'. What characterizes these idyllic events is the absence of bad feelings: jealousy, envy, persecution and hatred. And within them K is able to be entirely loving and entirely good; joined with her object in perfect goodness forever.

What I have been hoping to illustrate in this chapter is that period in an analysis when an initial rigorous and implacable splitting begins to soften; when it is possible for the patient to have momentary experiences of the goodness of a separate whole object.

It is at that moment that envy becomes most poisonous and dangerous, because as it destroys the goodness of the object, it prevents an introjection of, and partial identification with, the object in its goodness, and this impedes emotional growth and flexibility. But this level of destructive envy is also dangerous and destructive to the self by adding to a proliferation of bad feelings which then have to be projected and become the imagined or real provocateurs of persecution from the object.

This period in an analysis – when powerful envy has been released – is always very difficult, requiring both strength and sensitivity in the analyst.

References

Klein, M. (1940) Mourning and its Relation to Manic-Depressive States. In M. Klein, *Contributions to Psychoanalysis: 1921–1945*. London: Hogarth Press [1965].

Klein, M. (1946) Notes on Some Schizoid Mechanisms. In M. Klein, *Envy and Gratitude and Other Works: 1946–1963*. London: Hogarth Press [1975].

Klein, M. (1957) Envy and Gratitude. In M. Klein, *Envy and Gratitude and Other Works: 1946–1963*. London: Hogarth Press [1975].

Klein, M. (1963) On the Sense of Loneliness. In M. Klein, *Envy and Gratitude and Other Works: 1946–1963*. London: Hogarth Press [1975].

Likierman, M. (2001), *Melanie Klein: Her Work in Context*. London: Continuum.

Petot, J.-M. (1991) *Melanie Klein, Volume II: The Ego and the Object*. Madison, WI: International Universities Press.

6 Pity and Disconnection

The Misuse of Metaphor

Priscilla Roth

In his important study of Melanie Klein's work, Petot writes:

> When Klein undertook the psychoanalysis of [Dick] she found herself facing a fundamental obstacle which she describes in terms of a lack. He had no symbolic relationship with things, they had no emotional value for him and therefore when he manipulated objects, this strictly meant nothing; we cannot consider his play or activity as a symbolic representation with underlying fantasies.
>
> (Petot, 1991, p. 226)

Dick's one interest was in doors and door handles and the opening and shutting of them. Klein connected this to his phantasies about the penetration of the penis into the mother's body, and concluded that what had brought symbol-formation to a standstill was the dread of what would be done to him after he had penetrated into his mother's body.

Klein also noted that in early childhood one of Dick's symptoms had been a refusal to chew his food. Thus, as Petot describes, Klein's interpretation focused both on the equation between the inhibited actions and an oral-sadistic attack, and the paralysing nature of this equation: 'Dick's further development had come to grief because he could not bring into fantasy the sadistic relation to the mother's body'. Petot remarks:

> The obvious idea here is that Dick's incapacities arose not from a lack of meaning or of cathexis of reality but, on the contrary, from *too much meaning*. If fantasizing activity is suspended it is not in default of a certain symbolic relationship between biting to pieces and cutting with a knife; rather, it is because this relationship is *too* pregnant: to cut with a knife is, in the unconscious, so confused with 'attacking the breast with teeth' that Dick cannot let himself do it, any more than the patient in Hanna Segal's famous example could let himself play the violin in public. The symbol is so little differentiated from the thing symbolized that it cannot escape the inhibition affecting the latter.
>
> (Petot, 1991, p. 227)

DOI: 10.4324/9781003588870-8

Thus things cannot be used symbolically; they cannot have some qualities of – be like – the object. They *are* the object. This is, we know, a symbolic equation. What I am drawing attention to is Klein's suggestion that what looks like a lack of the capacity of symbol-formation in Dick should be understood not as an absence of meaning in the objects or the activities relating to them in the external world, but as the *'uncontrollable proliferation of their meanings'*.

According to Klein, what paralysed and impeded Dick's development was the too early and too considerable occurrence of a process in itself positive, that is, an 'identification with the object attacked'. Because of this too-early identification Dick could not bear his own aggression. Any aggressive action with toys or other objects was followed not only by anxiety but by feelings of guilt and pity and a feeling that he must make restitution. This too-early identification with his object led to a premature empathy, resulting in a confusion between persecutory anxiety and early feelings of guilt. In other words, a pre-mature confrontation with the complex anxieties of the depressive position.

And this is what I want to describe in the patient I will tell you about: an unmanageable identification with his attacked objects, threatening him with confusion and inhibiting his capacity to symbolize and to form relationships.

Like Dick, my adult patient, Mr W, had no interest in things of the world, they had no meaning for him. For the first few years in analysis, he manifested a great inhibition in any capacity to connect with anyone or anything with any depth of feeling – except in troubled ways with his parents and older brother and, in a peculiar and even fetishistic fascination with fine food.

In his poem 'Some Lines Composed on Tintern Abbey', Wordsworth illuminates the preciousness of the experience that 'in this moment there is life and food / For future years'. For my patient, such moments do not exist. 'Food' in Wordsworth's poem suggests (but isn't limited to) 'inspiration', 'nourishment', 'enrichment', 'sustenance', 'comfort'. 'Food' for my patient has been limited – concretely – to a reservation at 'the best restaurant in the world'.

What I hope to show in this paper are the initial, tentative signs of the emergence of an apprehension and appreciation of meaning in a patient for whom this had seemed impossible, and to venture some understanding of the still active impediments to its development, namely, the ongoing consequences of what I imagine to have been a premature confrontation with depressive anxieties. I am, like Klein, assuming the presence in my patient of a capacity for symbolic thought (so a functional, rather than an organic lack.), and that his inability to relate to people and things in a creative and imaginative way is a function not of the absence of their meaning to him, but of an over-abundance of meaning, as he becomes confused with his objects. These signs of some development are small and fleeting and only partial: in his more mature mind he is, I hope to show, beginning to form some attachments, to tolerate feeling some pity and some gratitude towards his objects. That is, some depressive capacities are beginning to emerge and develop. But there is at the same time a mad part of his mind that seems not to improve. A question posed by the work is whether these two worlds can ever be bridged.

In my essay 'The Unconscious Thread and the Here and Now' (Chapter 7, this volume) I stress the importance of understanding that the central unconscious phantasy, at its most fundamental level, only emerges, and its meaning can only be grappled with, after years of a long slow process in a psychoanalysis. There is no shortcut to this understanding. In this patient, underneath what is presented as an emotionally paralysed, thought-disordered person, are powerful unconscious phantasies about the nature of his object relationships, phantasies which are essential to understanding his otherwise peculiar restricted personality.

I couldn't describe my patient as psychotic, and he can certainly function in the practical world. But there are marked psychotic elements in his personality, and the world to which he is obliged to limit himself is narrow, circumscribed and concrete. He holds a job in finance in which he has no interest. Indeed, interestingly, his accumulated money also earns him no interest: he cannot invest – find interest in – things or people in the world; similarly, he cannot invest his money so that it might grow and provide – he cannot gain interest from any source. This idea (invest = invest) is what he calls a 'metaphor'. That is: (a) he has earned a lot of money and he is unable to invest that money. And (b) he is unable to take an interest in any kind of professional or social or emotional or even recreational activity. Hence, he says, 'a metaphor'. His use of this term in this way is an indication that Mr W has begun to notice, and even appreciate a little, that my way of working as an analyst is to put things together, to make links, and he wants to be able to do this himself. He has boiled down and summed up this way of thinking – thoughts linked to each other – as 'metaphor'. For Mr W, the concept of metaphor itself has lost most of its metaphorical meaning. 'It's a metaphor' he says frequently. Buying wine, he says, is a 'metaphor' for finding a girlfriend.

An essential quality of metaphor is how similarity and difference exist simultaneously; the metaphor and the metaphored each retain their own qualities, each adding something to the penumbra of meanings of the other. For my patient, metaphor means equivalence, sameness, replacing one with the other with nothing gained and nothing lost. It speaks of symbolic equation, not symbolization. Grappling with the confusion of two things being related but separate, differentiable, Mr W finds a word to concretize the idea. Metaphor.

Referred by his former analyst in Toronto, he consulted me because he was unable to get a girlfriend and because his relationship with his parents and his brother troubled him: he wished he didn't continuously feel so irritated with them and also worried about them. He is the second of two brothers. His father, now on the verge of retiring and suffering from depression, has always been a worry: he, father, lost his leg in an accident at the age of 16 and wears a cumbersome artificial leg. During the patient's childhood, his father had been an addicted gambler and had lost most of the family money. He had been bullying and aggressive to his wife and older son; my patient sees himself as always trying to be the peacemaker in the family. The patient's mother is seen as manipulative and intrusive, and emotionally dishonest. He deals with his fear of involvement with his parents – their intrusiveness, his irritation with them – by taking them on 'the best holiday of their life' each year.

Mr W told me two stories in the first weeks of the analysis which have returned repeatedly. The first was about an incident when he was a small boy at summer camp. One day, in a playful way, he had thrown a rock into the air which landed on the head of another boy. There had been a lot of blood, the boy was taken to hospital and the camp counsellors had been very angry with my patient. His parents had been sued and had had to pay money to the injured boy's parents. Until his early twenties my patient believed that he had either killed or brain damaged the child, and that his own parents were devastated and bankrupted by the lawsuit. When, in his twenties, he mentioned this to his parents, they were shocked: the boy had been fine, undamaged; they had not been terribly upset, they had sent $1000 to the boy's parents to cover ancillary costs. Their concern was with how much their own son, my patient, had suffered with these thoughts over the years.

The second story was ostensibly of lost love. In graduate school in Vancouver he'd fallen deeply in love with B and she with him. He admired everything about her, she 'made him a better person', they 'shared a commonality'. These ways of describing her – with a few hard-edged and neverchanging examples – were repeated in almost every session. The relationship ended because after some months he didn't want to 'sleep with' B anymore: he wasn't sexually attracted to her. Her ass was too big and her nose too bumpy. She was a great girl, a really great girl, but he thought he could do better: he'd find a prettier B. Having left her and moved to another city, he began to miss her and to feel he'd made a tremendous mistake. That, and his dissatisfaction with his job in a major financial institution, led him to seek analysis with Dr M. After a year of analysis he decided to leave his job and give himself over completely to 'exploring' himself and his 'options' – he was smitten with the idea of 'self-actualization'. He soon saw this as a terrible mistake: being jobless terrified him. In this state of mind, and panicking that he would never find another job, he had accepted a position in London.

Both these stories exist in historical reality and both speak of a powerful internal reality: irreparable damage, and the frailty of love in the face of it. As the analysis developed, the implications of the stories continued to take shape in my mind.

The most powerful impression I had of Mr W for some time was of an almost comical out-of-touch quality. I'll describe some of his attitudes and behaviours to give you a sense of him. He was my first patient in the mornings; when I arrived at the building, he was always waiting outside, texting or talking on his phone. As I would unlock the door, he would closely follow me, standing and walking inches behind me. As I took a step in, so he took a step-in step with my own. This was disconcerting. The sessions were characterized by endless streams of circular monologues, without pause, beginning the moment he lay down, and which could, if I let them, continue through the entire session. These monologues were repetitive and full of clichés – things like 'you gotta spin to win', and 'I'm just gonna throw something against the wall and see if it sticks'. In time it became clear that these uninterruptable monologues had two functions: first, he was convinced that I needed him to keep talking: that 'nothing would happen' if he stopped talking. At the same time, he felt he needed to keep talking in order to keep me from thinking anything that might be dangerous to him.

In these first years Mr W's romantic life consisted of brief encounters with women of whom he tired quickly or, more often, who were not interested in him. He thought of this in terms of catching a 'hot' enough girl. 'Hot' meant visibly so: girls who would make other people value him more highly. He considered adding an inch to his description of himself on an internet dating site and wondered whether this would be false advertising. He found it hard to understand why he was having trouble getting a hot girl, since, as he said, he's got a lot going for him: he makes quite a lot of money, he's not bad looking, he can tell you the names of all the great little bistros in Europe, and he knows more about Sushi than anyone in London. His description of his former relationship with B included examples of stunning insensitivity: he once told her that while other guys liked having flashy sports cars, he thought of her as a 'used car', which he didn't mind at all. He broke up with her, telling her he wasn't sexually attracted to her, but suggested that since he didn't have to leave town for a couple of months, they might keep up their relationship until he had to go.

With all this, there is something likeable, touching, about my patient; and, *gradually*, some things have begun to change: for the past year Mr W has been able to maintain a relationship with a woman, P, though this relationship, and its possible future, deeply troubles him: P, forty years old, wants to be married and to have children. She is a professional woman from a background similar to his own, and is what he describes as 'good-looking … not great-looking, but good-looking.' She knows he comes to analysis because he can't decide whether he can commit himself to her. This relationship represents a development not only in his external life but internally: he has begun to describe how pained he is when P says she loves him, since he cannot respond in the same way. He loves her, but he's not sure he's 'in love with' her. He puzzles about this and he worries not only on his own behalf but on hers. This is new.

And, whereas he used only to grab hold of my words and phrases as hard lumps of wisdom, repeating them back to me as if they were shared assumptions, he is now sometimes able to have more independently spontaneous thoughts of his own. Still, his way of learning largely remains concrete: he no longer asks 'Is P the one for me?', he asks 'Is P *a* one for me?'. He says 'If I broke up with P she would be devastated. That is a metaphor for my own feelings' and 'I am unplugged ... that is a metaphor for when I distance myself from P's problems to pass over my own.' He still desires to 'sleep with' all the pretty women he sees but he is aware that as soon as he has sexual intercourse with a woman, he loses interest in her – indeed, he is usually repulsed by her. Knowing this fills him with despair.

My patient has always attended his sessions religiously – he describes this in numerical terms: a larger number of sessions = a greater chance of faster progress; also, he's afraid he might miss a 'good' session (as opposed to a not-so-good session). He tries hard to get to all his sessions on time, often re-arranging business meetings at some professional risk to himself. My unwillingness to change a session time created some substantial resentment in the autumn and in response the patient accepted an invitation to a friend's wedding some weeks hence, and a trip to Toronto for Thanksgiving – both would involve missing sessions. He also began planning elaborate trips to take during my Christmas holidays – making sure he would be leaving on the last day I was working and not coming back until the morning of his first session back.

The patient's material is continuously and repetitively concerned with the difficult external situations he is in: Should he marry P? Should he leave his boring but lucrative job? and the pressure of these issues can seem to fill up the space for thinking. As we know, in analysis the transference is, for a long time, invisible and undetectable; to recognize its qualities requires allowing elements to play in one's mind, to coalesce and dissolve and gradually take form. This is largely an unconscious process. But once one begins to get a sense of the transference, and the powerful unconscious phantasies that are expressed within it, the external events which make up the patient's conscious material are mostly no longer seductive diversions, but instead take their proper place as part of the internal drama that is being played out within the analytic relationship.

I hope the material I will present will demonstrate this.

A Monday Session in Late October

He comes on time, as always. He is on his phone right into the waiting room and still looking at it, fiercely, as he comes into the room and lies down on the couch, at which point he clicks it off.

He says he is thinking about broadening his life ... and then without pause:

> I'm struggling with my relationship with P. She's a great girl, woman, I'm fortunate to have her, we ... what makes me ... challenges me ... she's crazy about me and also very loving, loyal ... a great woman. I'm torn because I'm quick to break out of relationships because of fears of being

in one, committing, something else not being there. I don't know when to stop looking, to settle.

Listening to him, on the one hand, I am aware that I have heard this many dozens of times. On the other hand, with another part of my mind I think that 'I don't know when to ... settle' is not just about a relationship with P but is about what happens to any relationship with anything: any thought or feeling. His fear of what happens when there is a connection between two, extends to every aspect of his life and every aspect of his thought. The 'struggle' he is having is right here and now, vitally in the very moment: he is struggling at every moment to stay in a relationship with his own thoughts – to keep them from being invaded and interrupted – and to stay in a safe-enough relationship with me. Trying to broaden his life.

> On the weekend, P gave a party. She used to party a lot, now three times a year, maybe. Dance music, drugs, we both had a lot of fun: she was DJ-ing, there were a lot of friends, we were both messed up, it was a good night ... as someone who's smoked in the past, not smoked for almost a year – I had maybe two cigarettes. We were happier because of the state we were in, but I was aware that we were really taking care of each other; it's a great relationship in so many ways: loving, we help each other, look after ... when I said I was going outside to get some fresh air for a minute she said 'I'll come with you'. The realization was – I said to her – of course this was affected by being on drugs – but I said to her, 'We really are a nice couple.'

Here each thought is qualified, reneged on, interfered with ... most espe-cially when he tries to express tender feelings: Thoughts such as 'we both had a lot of fun', 'it was a good night', 'we were really taking care of each other', 'we really are a nice couple' are continually punctuated by 'We were both messed up', 'of course we were happier because of the state we were in', 'of course this was all affected by being on drugs ...'

> I saw other girls at the party, pretty girls; I wanted to sleep with them, but I had a sense of appreciation of P. I'm very fortunate, I don't appreciate that sometimes. She's a great girl, woman. You never know what the future holds, what can happen to people, but if I was with her and my job ended, I'd be less scared, more prone not to do something stupid, like when I left Bank A. – because of the force of the other person. I always think you have more freedom in life when you have more money, less responsibility. But sometimes less attachments can put you in directions which are not for the best. October is our eleven-month anniversary. I'm trying to live in the moment. I'm scared about what can happen. Is marrying P right for me? I would have a better life with her – healthier. Having her at home: I've under appreciated how happy I've

been in the last year. I find I want to go over to her house, sleep next to her – nothing physical, just hold her. Just cuddle. I'm unsure. To say I could do worse is an understatement. I don't know who I am and who I will be which makes it hard, I don't know if I'm ready. She wants marriage, children, pretty quickly – if it was just marriage we could always separate if didn't work out, but … not with children. Also I don't know if there is something missing. I'm losing sexual interest. It seems to happen with all the women I'm with. R was a wonderful woman. There are many wonderful women in the world. By wonderful I mean honest, loyal. I hadn't smoked since December. I told P I had a cigarette, she said 'Well be careful'. I'm honest with her. Not like with my parents – I didn't tell them I smoked. The point is, with R it was wonderful – loyal, honest – with P, I have no concern she would betray me, be unfaithful, same with R, same with B.

He is expressing appreciation, good fortune – 'if I was with her I'd be less scared …' – and then 'I'm trying to live in the moment', which I think means trying to keep destructive forces out at this very moment as he tries to say something without being interfered with by his own doubts and attacks.

But, relentlessly, these forces come in and punctuate his thoughts: 'I'm scared … I want to sleep next to her but nothing physical', 'I'm unsure', 'I don't know if I'm ready', 'Could always separate', ' something missing', 'I'm losing sexual interest', 'Many wonderful women in the world'. And, interestingly, 'P is … not like my parents.'

What emerges is the obsessional doubt about the nature of his internal object and of his relationship with this object … will she betray me? Want something from me? Will I be trapped with her, in her, by her? Will I not love her? Wipe her out? Will she make me guilty? Am I bad?

All this is evident in his speech patterns – the breaking up of a link between one thought and the next – and in his description of his relationship with his girlfriend and powerfully, simultaneously, in that moment in the transference. For I am aware that as he is talking, he is struggling with a disturbing apprehension – just on the periphery of his awareness – of my presence and – thus far – my silence. ('I'm scared', 'I don't know if there is something missing', 'I'm unsure'). In a part of his mind, underlying everything else, of course P is his parents and I am his parents and all this is going on is between him and his internal object: loved, hated, attacked and feared, confused and confusing.

So, at this point I said to him that he has told me that he is struggling and I can see that he is; I said that he is trying to describe experiences of happiness and tenderness but they immediately get interfered with: qualified and diminished so he can't hold onto them.

He responded:

When you say that, it makes me think analysis does the opposite of what I think it is. That's the contrast I see between drugs and analysis: when you smoke a joint, you chill out. This [analysis] is where I work and sweat, grind through things, I'm mentally working. I sometimes wonder if analysis makes my mind more active. The whole point is talking about things. This is the forum where I do this. Vocalize. Only place I can let it all out. I generally have an active mind, I don't share that with anyone else. Here I vocalize and internalize in some place where I can see my own thoughts. I don't know how else analysis would work. Are you saying I've been doing it wrong for 4 years?

Something about my speaking has disturbed him. I have interfered with his struggle to maintain that he is all right on his own, doesn't need me to talk to him. Whatever it is, he has responded defensively: 'I work and sweat', 'I have an active mind'. I can do this by myself! 'Vocalizing' is not object related.

So now I said: 'There has just been a weekend. And now there are two of us in this room. I think when you come into the session after a weekend, you feel anxious: anxious about coming in, about wanting to talk to me – I think you don't know what to do about a disturbing awareness of me. When you become aware of me, you might have to be worried about being betrayed, let down … And you worry about what I think of what you are saying. I think it feels too disturbing to be aware of those worries – not knowing what you think and feel about being here and about wanting to talk to me. I think you want to be here with me and are afraid of being here with me.

'When you come in, you are full of anxieties from experiences over the weekend, but you can't allow yourself to know that you want to tell this all to me. That *there are* two people in the room. You do show me that you feel a tenderness about P – but that too makes you anxious.'

Pause.

I … yeah … I think that … I have an appreciation when I'm on drugs, a euphoria, that's always true, it's infrequent, maybe three times a year. P used to do it nightly, music scene for years. Now she's like me, we're good for each other. She doesn't party every night now. But the real experience I had with her – I have to correct this that you said – the real experience with her was the day after the party. Usually I would be hung over, we were … recovering, it's usually hard, but I was appreciating being with her that day. Lying in bed, close, comfortable. Yesterday I stayed at her house, I ordered take-out food, a great place I know how to order from – at my house we were waiting for the food for 50 minutes. Just the notion of her being with me was nice: she was by the fire. I was on the couch. I wanted her with me but I know she gets cold, so she likes to be near fire. She was warmed by fire. I could picture going to the party, coming back with some random girl, being alone on the couch by myself. Nothing of having someone. I notice I don't say 'Having P.' That's a problem.

Now, my patient's response, following my saying 'We are two people in the room', gets prefaced by caveats, but eventually he tells me about 'the real experience' the day after the party, when he was able to appreciate being with P. This is important: It is a description of P and himself, P in front of the fire, he on the couch. A perfect distance each from the other. Two people in the room.

It is at the same time a picture of him and me when, for a moment, he feels we can both exist: when he is neither filling up all the space in the room and in my mind, nor feeling in danger of my taking him over. Neither of us is on top, neither is underneath, nor is either alone and abandoned. I don't need him to fix me – I have my own fire to warm me. He can allow this to be so. He has just taken in, and for a moment understands, how it is possible for there to be two people in a room.

But then something happens and at this moment, just after he has described this ideal state of being, he says 'I notice I didn't say "P"'. This is a switch.

What I said to him was: I think that you are aware of feeling when you are here of something that can take place that is particular to you and me. It is a specific relationship. And that this feels dangerous, and you have to wipe it out. You do this – wipe it out – by thinking that you are 'vocalizing' – where you are the only person in the room, or by generalizing – where the specificity of this particular relationship – you and me – is extinguished.

There was a longish pause and I had the impression that he was thinking. When he spoke he said:

> What I feel bad about P is: I can't reciprocate her feelings. She is in love with me, wants to have children with me. I am struggling, not sure that she makes me feel as I really want to feel. She knows about my relationship issues, but we don't talk about it. She doesn't say the things she wants to say because I don't want to hear them – not because I don't like that she loves me but because it makes me feel bad – I can't feel the same. She is this great woman and at some point I will … She says 'I love you so much'. I say 'Yeah'. This makes me sad. Don't like when she says them because I struggle that I don't feel same way. Makes me guilty. As if I kick her to the curb. That's not what I feel, not what I want to do … She's so glad to see me when I come home! I don't know if I just don't feel the same way or am holding out for something better … One thing I will say is the relationship is healthy.

I think this is a response to my referring to feelings 'particular to you and me'. My patient suddenly feels I want him to love me, to take care of me. This frightens him, understandably, but it also makes him feel sad and guilty. He feels concerned for P – and perhaps for me – and he pities her that he can't return her love.

Between this session and the next I'll present, I was called away from London and cancelled two sessions.

Thursday, a Week Later

He tried to phone his parents last night; he's taking them away over Christmas, he was trying to figure out where:

> My mother didn't pick up [the phone]; I was happy about it, I have no energy to deal with it. I get concerned about what will happen when they get older: A's [his sister in law's] father has colon cancer, doesn't have long to live. I know this guy, a lawyer, he said his parents were okay to 82, then they went downhill. My parents are getting older; of course they are relatively healthy now. I won't know how to deal with it … gets me down. One thing, even though they may not like it, I have the financial ability to take care of them. I don't want to get old.

He was telling P about his colleague's wife (who was in hospital with possible brain damage). He told P that he doesn't want to live with brain damage. He doesn't want to be a vegetable. He wouldn't want to live. 'I can't live with being a burden.' P got upset. 'She cares about me. I don't know what to do.'

There's this guy he knows. The guy lost his job. Had a good job. About 50, 55: he's a 'putz', but a nice guy. Pain in the ass, but not a bad guy. Lost his job. He has kids, wife. 'What would I do? What will happen to me? It will be hard to find another job … realize I've gotta stay in my job, make sure I make enough money. Don't know what I will do.'

'We were thinking of going to Alba for truffle season, thought it would be fun, but … there's just too much travelling, too expensive, I didn't really feel like it.' So, he ordered it all for home: he cooked an all-truffle dinner for some of P's friends: every course had truffles in it. The guy said it was the best dinner he's ever had. He bought the truffles from Selfridges: 'I got a great deal, 15% off because it was a slightly older supply. So, I bought them all. P's friends were effusive. I have a nice place, I put some good music on; three, four courses, it was way beyond nice. And not at a restaurant. It's what I should be doing. It took a lot of care, it was a pain in the ass, but … I enjoy it when people say "This is amazing!" I'm someone who likes praise and admiration for what I do. That's the part I like – not the work. I'd never want to do it all the time.' Pause. 'I could be a doctor, I'd like to help people; I could be an artist, or a musician … but I'll just do it in my spare time. I like to be praised. But I need the money … I don't want to be a starving artist.'

I said to him:

> I think you wish you knew what to do to make me say 'amazing' about you, like you want to do for your parents. You want desperately to feel you can take care of them – do things which make you feel you are good: be a doctor or make a wonderful dinner; provide for your parents and make them better. And make me better when you are worried about

me. You are excited that you didn't need to go out to the restaurant – you want to be the restaurant: making the amazing dinner. And you wish that you didn't need to come to this room for help – you wish that you could be your own analyst. This is particularly powerful right now because next week you will be missing sessions – and there are breaks ahead, and it makes you panicky. And then things feel like they are falling apart – you don't know if anyone is alright, not P or your parents or me or you.

Pause.

'Don't forget I've been there. I threw myself off the cliff.' (He is referring to the time he left his good job in Toronto.) 'I was crazy to think I had the power to do something I couldn't do. But I've learned things, now I have a degree of pragmatism. Change will come when it comes. You have to appreciate I have some experience in that way of thinking.' Silence. 'I don't know what to … do I not want to change? This whole thing may be a waste of time.'

Silence.

I said:

When you get panicky about being on your own next week, afraid that you won't be able to be your own analyst, you feel everything will fall apart. It feels terrifying. You get afraid you won't be able to take care of anyone – you think that if you can't feel amazing that you won't be able to fix your parents and that they will die and that then you will starve and die. And when you feel like this, everything feels a waste – everything turns into waste.

He responded:

Yeah. I have tremendous concern about being with P. Should I be with P or not be with P? Am I being selfish? With R I knew it wouldn't work so finally got rid of … P made it past the point of a relationship brush-off. P got through the pattern … do I know the answer?

He went on about this for several minutes: should he, shouldn't he stay with P? I said:

I think that what I just said to you about your panic and confusion frightened you – it pushed into your mind the separations coming up. I think now you hope you can keep things safe in your mind and here between us, the same way you try to manage things with P: facing the break between us, you don't want me to say anything that feels disturbing, you hope that we can have a kind of safe companionship.

Discussion

A phrase repeats itself throughout this material: 'I don't know what to do', 'What will I do?', 'What will happen to me?'. At the beginning of the session, my patient is painfully identified with internal objects in a precarious state: people are falling apart, his parents are getting older, people are dying. He's worried about what caused my absence. His objects' frailties and damages have become his own, so deeply is he identified with them. These identifications are fluid and persecuting and, in a terrifying way, he becomes each character in the story, melts into each one as each melts into the other: his father becomes his sister-in-law's father, becomes him. He becomes his colleague's brain-damaged wife, then becomes 'this guy he knows' who's lost his job. In this *'uncontrollable proliferation of meanings'* his own personality deliquesces, frighteningly. He reminds himself that he financially looks after his parents: since he and his objects are the same, if he doesn't support his parents, cure them, keep them alive, they will die and therefore he will die. If he can't keep me alive he will die. This is terrifying. His solution to this is another, more massive attempt at projective identification with a perfect and perfectly omnipotent object.

This is what the truffle dinner material is about: he will deal with his panic about being left alone by becoming the owner of the restaurant – the provider of all the truffles in the shop.

But his projective identification with this version of me can't be maintained: the mania fails, and he's left in a desperate state. This is what he's referring to later in the session when he points out that he's 'been there' – the time when, in a manic state – in love with the idea of 'self-realization', he quit his job and immediately fell into a paralysing depression.

In this precarious organization, any imperfection in the object is experienced as damage (the story he told of B's too-big ass), and any damage is experienced as catastrophic (the story of his throwing the rock). The experience is catastrophic because it confronts him with a depressive anxiety that quickly turns into an intolerable persecution: you could say that *my patient suffers from the cruelty of the imperfect object*. The anxieties he faces are both depressive: he has destroyed the ideal object, which is now in terrible pain, is impoverished, is helpless, will die if he cannot repair it; and persecutory: in its imperfection, its damage, it has become a bad object and it cruelly attacks him by depriving him of the perfect object and thus of being able to love; leaving him filled instead with hatred and contempt.

At the same time, the ever-present danger of his identification with the catastrophically damaged object is immediate and terrifying. Either he can keep the parents alive and well forever or they will die and he will die. Everything he tries is a waste.

This is persecution and, at the same time, depressive anxiety: 'the situation in which all one's loved ones within are dead and destroyed, all goodness is dispersed, lost, in fragments, wasted and scattered to the winds; nothing is left within but utter desolation ...' (Riviere, 1936, p. 313).

'What am I supposed to do?' he asks.

But he is struggling. Every once in a while in a session he gets a glimpse of another way: an experience of him on the couch and me by the fire: that is, some sense of equilibrium, before the disappointment, resentment and destruction take over: before I demand that he be perfectly loving, and he can't be; and he demands that I be perfectly perfect and I can't be.

When I interpret his desperation, he is sometimes more reassured that I am not either empty or vengeful, that I understand that he is in a place of despair: 'What am I supposed to do?' he asks again.

These are my observations of my patient. They seem to me to suggest a pervasive unconscious phantasy containing overwhelming depressive as well as persecutory elements, dominating and underlying everything he thinks and does. Following Klein's description of her treatment of Dick (Klein, 1930), I find myself imagining that a premature and therefore unmanageable confrontation with depressive anxieties – at a time when persecutory anxieties had not yet diminished – led in my patient's development to rapid over- identifications with his aggressed against objects, inhibiting symbolization and sublimation and interfering profoundly with his development.

To return to Dick: looking at some *pencil shavings* in Mrs Klein's lap one day, Dick saw *his analyst* in fragments ... and pitied her. 'Poor Mrs Klein', said Dick.

Things which seem to be meaningless in fact may have too much meaning.

References

Klein, M. (1930) The Importance of Symbol-Formation in the Development of the Ego. *International Journal of Psychoanalysis* 11: 24–39.

Petot, J.-M. (1991) From Sadisms to Reparation Mechanisms. In J.-M. Petot, *Melanie Klein, Volume I: First Discoveries and First System 1919–1932*. Madison, WI: International Universities Press.

Riviere, J. (1936). A Contribution to the Analysis of the Negative Therapeutic Reaction. *International Journal of Psychoanalysis* 17: 304–320.

Segal, H. (1957) Notes on Symbol Formation. *International Journal of Psychoanalysis* 38: 391–397.

7 The Unconscious Thread and the Here and Now

Priscilla Roth

David Foster Wallace, an American novelist who died in 2008, began a lecture three years before his death by telling a story. The story seems to suit my purpose too, so I will quote him:

> There are these two young fish swimming along, and they happen to meet an older fish swimming the other way, who nods at them and says, 'Morning boys, how's the water?' And the two young fish swim on for a bit and then eventually one of them looks over at the other and says, 'What the hell is water?'
>
> (Wallace, 2009)

The psychoanalytic concept of the Here and Now describes a paradox, referring, as it does, to the near impossibility of actually being in the Here and Now; referring, in fact, to the way that what goes on in the current situation in an analysis repeats, re-instates, drags in, replays a There and Then: the repetitive, unchanging dominant phantasy in the patient's (and sometimes of course the analyst's) life. Indeed, moments when a patient in analysis can, for however short a time, be and know he is in the Here and Now – the present, with a person who is his psychoanalyst, are rare. Mostly moments that look like a different kind of perception of the analytic engagement are themselves largely defensive, intellectualized movements within a transference relationship – that is to say, within a relationship here and now that has its roots in and replays a there and then.

I want to differentiate between two things: between, on the one hand, a conviction that an analytic patient's most fundamental internal object relationships, existing as unconscious phantasies, will always be manifested within a transference relationship with his analyst, provided that the analyst protects the analytic structure which allows this to be so. This is a conviction I'll assume many of us share and it has been well described over the years.

But I think it is necessary to differentiate this essential recognition of an empirical truth from the idea that one can therefore always, in every or even most sessions, from early on in an analysis, be aware of what the nature of this transference is: be aware of the content and quality and particular

DOI: 10.4324/9781003588870-9

distinguishing characteristics that make the patient's central dominating phantasies so essential to his personality and so pervasive in all his relationships. More often, for a long time, we are both, patient and analyst, swimming in a medium we do not recognize, cannot identify, and, indeed, whose existence we are not even aware of. It takes a long time to get a convincing picture of a patient's dominant unconscious phantasy: what we as analysts do along the way is critical to this endeavour and must, first of all, ensure that we are not interfering with its emergence into the transference or with our own gradually developing awareness of it. Sometimes we may pay such close attention to what we feel our patients are doing from moment to moment in the session that we fail to pay attention to the underlying story and hence miss an opportunity to identify it.

There are phantasies and phantasies. We all have phantasies all the time; they influence and skew our perceptions and experiences, tying our present to our past. But we all have more central phantasies which can completely determine the way we see the world, intruding on our ability to learn and to relate to new events. These are more primitive, more deeply unconscious, more fundamental phantasies which may never reach consciousness but whose derivatives appear in enactments both in and out of the analysis – in dreams and powerfully but often concealed, within transference and counter-transference experiences. I think of a central determining phantasy existing for each individual, lying deeply unconscious and affecting that person's attitudes, colouring everything that takes place whether we recognize it or not.

Such deeply unconscious phantasies are, like the water the fishes swim in, invisible and impossible to apprehend, at least for a long time. It is the presence of these phantasies that creates the transference of the total situation. (Joseph, 1985; Klein, 1952).

K came to analysis in her early thirties, anxious about her inability to form a lasting relationship with a man. Beautiful and accomplished, she had come to the UK from the US, to pursue graduate studies. K has two younger sisters, both are married and one has two children.

I will describe K's analysis and how it developed because it is a story of how two fish – a patient and an analyst – spent a long-time swimming in an element they were not aware of.

Several things stand out in my mind about the first year or so of the analysis. There was an idealized transference: she was relieved to be in analysis and had high hopes that it would help her. There was a particular quality to her material; it had no actual manifest content but was instead a kind of running commentary on her feelings: 'Yesterday afternoon I didn't feel so good, but later I felt better', or the reverse, sometimes in great detail about the hour-by-hour changes in her feelings without giving me any information about anything that was going on in her life. My sense was that there was to be nothing for my mind to hook onto separate from her feelings as she described them. I also noticed her way of repeatedly referring to 'my analysis'; something about the way she said it made me feel it didn't have anything to do with me. Also, right from the beginning she often spoke about the 'progress' she was making in her analysis; I was aware that this too had a meaning I couldn't understand.

In these first couple of years she dated several young men without anything serious developing between them. Then, one Monday, she reported that she was in love: she had gone out with a young man, B, on Thursday evening and they had liked each other so much that they'd spent the whole weekend together. She had never felt this way before, she thought he felt the same. For that week she was extremely happy, describing his fine qualities and the wonderful way he made her feel. Then the complaints started. Two weeks after the first date she began complaining that he wasn't sufficiently 'committed' to 'the relationship'. He did not behave the way a boyfriend was supposed to behave: he did not send her sweet texts during the day, or go around and open the car door for her as other boyfriends do. Or 'whisk her off to Paris for a weekend'. He didn't make tapes of the songs they'd heard together or even remember that they had heard certain songs together.

These were not minor irritations, which she might laugh about or feel a little ashamed of feeling. These were accusations of a major order; her complaint was 'Why do I have to have *this* relationship? Why can't he be a better boyfriend? Why can't I have the relationship I want?' Partly this was to do with what she was convinced her friends had, but mainly it expressed the conviction that B had the ability to give her what she wanted, and he just wasn't doing it.

There was something odd about her complaints: they were never about anything obviously substantive in the real world, and as they continued and increased, I sometimes felt irritated, but I always felt puzzled and curious about what was behind them. In the analysis K insisted that my sole job was to facilitate 'my relationship': to understand how impossible it was that B behaved the way he did, and to keep her on an even keel so that she didn't ruin 'the relationship'. When I tried to address what this was indicating about her and me – the analytic relationship – she insisted, 'I don't want to talk about YOU! I want to talk about my relationship.' She was furious about my holiday break, but only because it put her in a bad mood and that had impacted on her relationship.

I am making two points here: the first is that the thing she called 'my relationship' was – and this was true also for 'my analysis' – a concrete thing; a boyfriend was a person who was supposed to bring her 'boyfriend-ness', relationship-y things, as I was supposed to bring her 'progress'. And while her complaints did not appear to be substantive (in the real world as I said above), I was increasingly sure that at a different level these complaints were real and meaningful. And not fundamentally about B.

My second point is to emphasize that the atmosphere in the analysis had become one of constant anger, disappointment, failure and blame. This was to continue in different forms for a long time.

K and B married about eighteen months after they met. The analysis continued to be filled with complaints about him and self-justifying reports of her screaming attacks on him. During this time I tried to understand and speak to her about her projections into B of hated and shameful parts of herself and then, more consistently, about her hatred of his separateness from her. It was difficult for me to find a way to convey to her my own sense of being, on the one hand, completely necessary to her well-being, and, on the other, repeatedly pushed away from any emotional contact with her. 'My analysis' definitely did not mean a deepening relationship with her analyst; it meant something like my giving her a thing she called 'progress' so she could have the things she wanted to have in her life. I believe the interpretations I made were mostly correct as far as they went, and sometimes they could be meaningfully linked with particular experiences in the transference – her response to a holiday or her fury about something new appearing in the consulting room. But for a long time the heat of her attention was entirely on 'the relationship' and my attempts to explore her relationship with me were met with disdain. This meant that I had all the time to bear the experience of feeling some contact had been made between us, only to find myself reminded of how inconsequential I was.

During this period what she took away from the work we were doing was equally concrete: the idea that she shouldn't attack her husband because it was strategically not a good thing to do – she might lose him – and, though much more slowly, because it began to make her feel guilty.

She was trying to be 'better' which meant to behave better, but all sorts of situations would suddenly precipitate a rage that she couldn't control. The most frequent was something that might have seemed innocuous: when she was in their flat and B came home from work, the moment she heard his voice, or caught sight of him, she felt furious. And the other way around: when she came home and first saw him in the flat she was filled with rage. I began to understand that her fury was that he had not been there all along.

One day she reported that the previous night B had offered to make dinner for her. She was pleased about his offer. He cooked fish and vegetables – she'd told him how to do each   and they were okay but – with tremendous disappointment – he didn't time it right: the fish was done perfectly several minutes before the vegetables were perfectly cooked, so the fish had to wait and the whole dinner was spoiled for her. She told this story with a mixture of anger at B and a kind of self-loathing – Why did he do it that way, and why should I mind so much? Both parts of the question troubled her; I felt her question about herself was a sign of some progress.

She began increasingly to have rages with me that were similar to what happened when she met B at their flat: simply seeing me at the waiting room door would create a 'bad mood' – she'd been fine on the way to her session, but as soon as she saw me she felt angry. I told her the dates of a short break two and a half weeks before the break: she was furious not because of the break itself, which she knew was on the cards, but because she was certain that I had known what the dates were some time before I'd told her about them. It wasn't possible that I hadn't known before I'd told her. I could have – I should have – told her earlier. Similarly, a small new item on a shelf in the consulting room brought rage: I must have decided to bring it in before she saw it – she hadn't known. She screamed 'It IS humiliating!' This change – in which at least sometimes the focus of her disturbance was the analytic relationship, made her sessions more obviously difficult but also made them more alive.

Sometimes she would be so angry that she was unable to lie down on the couch. Sitting up on its edge, I could see her making faces, rolling her eyes sarcastically, contemptuously looking up to the ceiling while jutting out her lower jaw, twirling her foot, earnestly studying her fingernails – a conjunction of activities which always felt like a mad conversation she was having with herself from which I was completely excluded, except that I had to observe it and I had to mind. But interpretations along these lines always increased her sense of alienation – she was trying to be 'good' but I always seemed to find a way to tell her what she wasn't doing right.

For awhile I saw this as just the newest development of the familiar picture: when she wasn't attacking herself in the analysis and wasn't attacking B to me ('he tells me I make him feel inadequate; he IS inadequate') – completely justifying the attacks and completely identified with the attacker of him, K was attacking me for what she felt were my constant attacks on her. All these sessions, filled with complaints about B or me or herself had the same quality: disappointment, fault and blame. *This* complaint – all I do is attack her, criticize her – increased over a couple of months and the sessions became very difficult. I could understand that what we were dealing with were further movements of a most cruel superego: having been directed at B and at me, and then at herself, this superego now seemed immovably located in me and it threatened the continuation of the analysis itself.

She decided that as she had made a lot of 'progress' – she had wanted to be married and now she was – there wasn't any reason to stay in analysis any longer. She began to insist on setting a leaving date. In any case, she didn't think analysis was helping her anymore; I only ever talked about her problems, her faults; why couldn't I talk about how much progress she had made? Why didn't I tell her how well she handled a conversation with a colleague or a visit with her mother? 'Normal' people didn't need analysis – was I telling her she was not normal? The interpretations I made became dangerous things – and they infuriated her – because they always implied that she was not okay, would never be 'normal', would 'screw up' her future children as her parents had screwed her up. 'Everything you say is a criticism,' she said, 'otherwise you wouldn't say it. Everything you say is telling me I haven't got it right. You may not think that is true, you may think you are being helpful and just pointing things out. I think you probably do think that. *But if there is something to point out, you are being critical; telling me I am not good enough.*'

Having set a date for when she would end her analysis, she came to a session and remarked that builders were coming to do some repairs to her house and she was worried that they wouldn't be finished with the work in time. I said I thought she was anxious about the work we still need to do and frightened that we won't be able to do what she needs before the date she's set to stop. 'NO! No!' she shouted, 'When I hear you say that, all I can hear is you saying "You're not ready. Your mind is full of crap." That's not what I said! You're telling me I should be worried about my mind. You're putting me down! That's not what I'm talking about.'

I said I understand she feels I am putting her down, but I was talking about what I think is her anxiety, a real worry, I thought, about whether there is enough time for some building inside her to take place.

She responded, 'When you say what you say, you make me feel you're saying, "Can't you see how you can't cope? You're always going to be persecuted by dirty builders, by dust."'

Still later she described a young mother she saw on the bus whose baby was lying flat on her lap. She was worried about the baby because the mother wasn't picking the baby up and holding him.

I said that if I say to her that she needs me to pick her up properly – to understand her, to hold onto what she feels, to help her feel safe – she will feel I am criticizing her.

She said:

> Yes. I feel that to be a criticism. That I'm not holding on to what said. That I won't stay with it. I think that is a criticism. I've been told I've done something wrong. That's all I can hear. If you pointed out something positive I wouldn't feel criticized. You always say that I can't stand you pointing out something I don't know. It's not right. Praise, agreement, a new idea … the things you say are critical, they're not just your thoughts, they always mean there is room for improvement. If you said, 'That's interesting … that thing you said; it shows you are feeling positive and capable', I wouldn't feel criticized even if I hadn't thought it. Or if you said, 'it seems like you are recognizing similarities in the way you approach different situations and deprive yourself', that's not a criticism. What you say are criticisms, not just your thoughts. Things you consider anti-intimacy – let's not pretend they're not criticizing, that they're just 'interesting'. They are saying I'm rubbish, that you hate me, that I shouldn't be doing that. You're not saying 'Poor you, you need to be held'; I can't feel that. Even if that's what you think you're doing. I'm not sure it is what you feel you're doing, but even if it is, I don't feel that. It's the nature of your job. Pointing out things I do that are moving away from an ideal.

'Pointing out things that are moving away from an ideal.'

My first reaction was to feel a frustrated sense of being again misunderstood. But I also had a feeling I couldn't shake that K was trying to communicate something to me which I hadn't understood. As I puzzled over some sessions in my mind, I found myself thinking about what was going on in a different way: from her point of view. I realized that from her point of view I was criticizing her. This was a sobering moment – the realization that, looked at through her eyes, things appeared very different. The recognition of this marked a change, a sea change, in my understanding. It was hard to do – it meant letting go of my secure position. But the change meant that something became possible that hadn't been possible before.

I understood that with each interpretation, each comment, I was saying what to her felt like 'You should be different. There is a better way – my way – and so long as you don't do it my way there will be a mismatch between what I think and what you are'. I was 'pointing out things that were moving away from an ideal'. I had to wonder why K was hearing me in that way; what made it so impossible for her to hear interpretations as attempts to understand, beginning of course with an examination of my own participation by tone or content. But I began then to reconsider K's disappointment and anger with her husband and with me and – with this small but highly significant turn of the kaleidoscope – I began to see that what had appeared manifestly in the analysis as a negative transference of failure and disappointment, could be understood as parts of a different picture. I was becoming aware of the water we had been swimming in.

I want to emphasize that I am not saying that I ought to have seen this picture earlier. My point is that all the experiences of the analysis had to be lived through before I could reach a point where the elements could rearrange themselves into a different shape in my mind, enabling a different picture to emerge.

I began to understand that my patient has a compelling and pervasive unconscious phantasy of a perfect union with her object, something called 'my relationship' which she unquestioningly knows exists somewhere and which is being kept from her by an object who continuously deprives her of it. Seen in this light, her husband's refusal to do things right is a cruel torture. She knows he could make her perfectly happy, be a perfect fit with her; she has evidence of it; after all, she felt it that whole first weekend. She has proof, too, that I can be right for her; she tells me she used to think I was 'wonderful'. 'Wonderful' is important: for her, its synonym is 'perfect'. It means that sometimes – if only for a split second – we had been felt to be exactly matched, perfectly fitting together. And 'perfect' equals 'normal'. Normal people, everyone else but her, have this perfect matching of expectation and reality all the time. The cruelty she is faced with, then, is a constant and at every moment current absolute conviction that the presence of the ideal object – the ideal relationship – is possible, and that every second of every session when we are not exactly together, exactly combined, is experienced as Not It: it is not here, not now; it is somewhere else. Each interpretation, then, is felt by definition to be marking the difference between her and me: you are there, I am here. *Telling her she has been moving away from the ideal.*

The unbearable lack of perfect synchronicity between the fish and the vegetables repeats itself in myriad ways; her sudden bad mood when she gets to a session to find we haven't been together until that moment, her rage when I tell her about an analytic break: the idea must have existed in my mind before I told her about it. And this must always be so: every thought I have must exist in my mind before she knows it and, as such, is a cruel display of her expulsion from the place where we could be together. In this longed-for place, the moment a thought is in my mind, she would also know it. The moment the ideal object exists, the ideal baby-herself is created. Knowing that there is a place where such a relationship exists, everywhere that is not this place means failure to her. I have failed to give it to her: she has failed to be good enough – perfect – to have it.

Talking to her about this phantasy, as it became more obvious within the analysis, brought important changes over the following months.

Moving Forward

Some weeks later K had a dream that she picked up the telephone to make a phone call, and, before she could even dial, she could hear, on the phone, the couple in the next door flat to hers 'shagging'. She put the receiver down, waited, picked it up again and still, all she could hear was the couple shagging – as if they were always shagging and would always be shagging every time she listened.

We talked about this dream. I said that in one corner of her mind there is a couple who are always, forever, every second, together – every time she picks up the receiver – every second of every day. I felt she understood. Now when I observed her sitting up on the couch, making contemptuous faces, rolling her eyes to the ceiling, seemingly having a conversation with herself in her mind, as I described earlier, I understood that I was watching her being a couple in intercourse. I thought the primary aim was the projection into me – the excluded onlooker – of impossible envious rage; that what I was viewing was a total intrusion of the primal scene with which she was in projective identification (Sodré, 2015).

In a session several weeks later, K described the garden in the house she grew up in. It was a beautiful garden, she said. There were flowering plants, beautiful trees and arbours of grapes. There was a pond behind the garden and a children's play area. She and her sisters used to play on the swings and climb on the arbour and throw things into neighbours' gardens. She doesn't remember her parents ever being in the garden. She can remember her father, he would be watering the lawn, the lawn was very important to him. But she has no memory of her mother there. She doesn't have a picture of her mother playing with them in the garden or anywhere. She can only picture her mother in the kitchen.

I think it's important that this vivid memory came into the analysis several weeks after the 'shagging dream' and our discussion of it: this was a different picture of a family and her place in it. It is a much saner fantasy. She has moved – at least at that moment – from the horror of the shagging dream with the omni-presence of the inseparable parental couple – to being an ordinary latency little girl, in love with her daddy while mother is safely in the kitchen. The liveliness in this picture illustrates my sense of increasing liveliness and space and growth in the analysis. This gave a picture of moving forwards.

Some weeks later, K went on holiday to X, a place she'd never been to before. She returned in a state of deep depression at having left it: she told me it was the only place where she'd ever felt she belonged. She couldn't explain why. She described the warmth of the sunshine, the friendliness of the people, but most of all a sense of having finally been absolutely where she belonged, where she was supposed to be. Her pain was acute and real. For a few sessions following her return she remained in this state of desolation.

I spoke to her about my understanding of her despair. I said that she was beginning to be able to recognize an enchanted place which she could be in during her holiday, but that it is an idealized place which she can have in her phantasy but she can't have in the real world. In the real-world people will always be moving away from her idea of the ideal – her idea of perfection. I said I thought she is beginning to realize that she can't have this in reality with real people but when she feels expelled from it – like now – when she finds herself in her ordinary real surrounding, it is painful. It is having to face the reality of reality.

Towards the end of the week she reported that she had begun to feel better, that her work was starting to interest her again and that she was being nicer to her husband who had been supportive about her distress.

K was beginning to know that this place where she felt she 'really belonged' was a place in her fantasies, her daydreams. And then she wakes up and goes through a profound but in fact a very transient depression.

That night she had a dream, it was similar to many dreams she has had during the analysis: in these dreams she is being chased by men who want to hurt her in some way: attack her, rape her, kill her. They lock her up and won't let her go. *In the dream of this particular night, she manages to escape from the man and run away; he comes after her and catches her and she is aware that he will punish her viciously for attempting to escape.*

I said to her that we had begun to understand that there is something inside her – a cruel and relentlessly punishing voice – which presents itself as protective – seducing her with the idea of paradise, insisting that she must only settle for perfect paradise. This voice in her is actually cruel and entrapping. When she can get a little bit freer from it, this seductive part of her – the man in the dream – is enraged at her freedom from it and re-doubles its attacks on her. This is the way this very powerful phantasy attempts to keep her chained to it, punishing and torturing her.

I felt she was understanding me.

So, things had moved. There was now a battle in her mind between a part of her who at some moments could feel allied with me in the analytic endeavour and close to her husband and able to get some pleasure from her life, and a part of her – in the dream called 'the man' – who will do anything to keep her trapped in her delusion. The battle was new and her awareness of it was a sign of a change in her.

And then she had what she said was a 'terrible dream'. She was in her parents' house but not the house she grew up in. B was sitting on the floor with his legs splayed, apart. His trousers were torn in the crotch and there was a big hole running down and blood was coming out of the hole. He looked at her with such sad eyes, as if he was saying 'I'm sorry, I'm sorry I can't help you.'. She woke up crying.

This is a terrifying picture of her object at the moment she becomes aware of its separateness from her. Originally her mother, in the dream her husband, it is now about her analyst as she contemplates leaving her analysis. Helpless and impotent, torn, weeping and bloody, the image reflects a recognition of the damage she has done. She has attacked – but not destroyed – the goodness of the object. This is something very new. The good mother/analyst is sad for her – sad that she can't help her. The mother, terribly sad for her child, is a moving image at the time of the separation. This is a new image. The dream is truly terrifying, but it is much more than that: it's a dream full of grief and sorrow.

Conclusion

The necessarily very gradual emergence into the analyst's conscious mind of the 'total situation' within the transference, which I am equating with a dominant phantasy, requires patience, time and what Bion (1978) called 'disciplined curiosity'. I understand this to imply a continuing awareness that what is taking place in an analysis demands a fluidity of perspective so that we can continually observe what is happening in the here and now of the session, and gradually begin to distinguish these moment-to-moment movements from the underlying substance in which the movements take place. There is no shortcut to this point – the point at which we can begin to differentiate the swimmers from the water.

References

Bion, W. (1978) São Paulo Seminar. In W. Bion, *Clinical Seminars and Other Works*. London: Karnac [1994].

Joseph, B. (1985) Transference: The Total Situation. In M. Feldman and E. Spillius (eds), *Psychic Equilibrium and Psychic Change*. London: Routledge in association with the Institute of Psychoanalysis.

Klein, M. (1952) The Origins of Transference. In M. Klein, *The Writings of Melanie Klein Volume 3: Envy and Gratitude and Other Works* (pp. 61–93). London: Hogarth Press [1975].

Sodré, I. (2015) The Perpetual Orgy: Hysterical Phantasies, Bisexuality and the Question of Bad Faith. In P. Roth (ed.), *Imaginary Existences: A Psychoanalytic Exploration of Phantasy, Fiction, Dreams and Daydreams*. London: Routledge in association with the Institute of Psychoanalysis.

Wallace, D. F. (2009) *This Is Water: Some Thoughts, Delivered on a Significant Occasion, about Living a Compassionate Life*. [Text of Commencement Speech at Kenyon College, 21 May 2005.] New York: Little, Brown.

Part II
Lectures and Essay

8   The Oedipus Complex Can Never Be Fully Dissolved

Priscilla Roth

My proposition today is that Freud's contention that the Oedipus complex is not simply repressed but permanently dissolved, destroyed and abolished can no longer be accepted as valid. I'll begin my argument with a clinical example.

A married couple came to consult with me. In their late forties, successful professionals, each had had years of analysis, and they had what until a few months before had seemed a successful marriage with three children. They had faced a number of more or less ordinary problems in their life together and had weathered them. So, the crisis which struck the pair when their youngest child – a boy – became adolescent was not happening to inexperienced or obviously disturbed parents. And that's why it was so surprising to them.

Both in individual therapy, they asked if they could come together to talk to me about the predicament in which they felt hopelessly stuck. The emails they sent described furiously stormy scenes at home, and, asking for help, revealed a total mutual incomprehension between them.

When we met, each – in great distress – related their view of the situation.

Mrs X felt two different things. Primarily, she felt she had to protect her child, now fourteen, against her husband's violent rage. She described her husband as rivalrous and attacking, and saw the child as his victim. Secondly, she felt completely tormented by the boy: although she tried to help him with his problems with friends or with school, he saw everything she did as completely useless. She was terrified about his depression, but also persecuted by his complaints and accusations against her husband: 'How could you be married to this horrible man? Why do I have to have this father?' So, Mrs X was in a desperate conflict. Her most powerful feeling was 'My heart is breaking at the sight of this child who has a cruel and terrible father'. This was the *cri de coeur* that dominated the picture. But alongside this was the other feeling: 'I'm being tormented by this child who hates his father and is ruining my marriage'. In this second picture the child is terrible both to his father and to her – to the couple. So, she is also persecuted by a child who – in her mind – is a bad child who is ruining a marriage, and in this position she feels sorry for his father and for herself.

This all feels completely unresolvable. Mrs X feels desperate and panicky: afraid her son will break down – be depressed, be mad, never go to school

DOI: 10.4324/9781003588870-11

again, never be a normal boy. Afraid he'll hate his father forever. And afraid the father will break down, and afraid the marriage will break up and the family be destroyed.

This is a mother in a massive identification with an Oedipal child. The identification goes far enough that she can actually think it would be better for the father to leave the family than for the child to suffer so from his presence. Though, as an adult, she loves her husband, she is so identified with the child that she loses the point of view of her husband and loses her own grown-up point of view. For Mrs X his problem is completely real – and completely in the *here* and the *now*: that this Oedipal situation must lead to the destruction of someone: the death of the marriage, the madness of one of the triangle. It is insoluble.

Mr X is equally agonized about the situation – from his point of view the boy's problems are entirely created by the fact that his mother spoils him, completely takes his point of view, and puts no boundaries between herself and her son. He believes in a father's absolute authority – as his own father did. The son needs to obey the rules or else he will be punished – as father himself was as a boy. And yes, he has hit him – once – the boy made him so angry. So: a man, suffering tremendously, and trapped in an identification with his own authoritarian father.

Both parents feel: 'This boy is going to break up our marriage'. Mother is desperate on behalf of her troubled child; father feels abandoned by mother who seems to love only their son. It feels to everyone, including the boy, that there is no solution, that life will always be a nightmare. The parents are completely polarized. Father says, 'He has to respect authority, he can't be allowed not go to school, he's got to study or he will be grounded.' Mother says, 'Surely it is better for him that we are completely understanding of him – he's depressed, he has no friends, he's suffering … why should he go to school this year? He can go next year. And why shouldn't he have blue and pink hair?' Father says: 'My son is going to school and my son is not going to have blue and pink hair.'

Each, too, is completely certain about their picture of the other: She knows that her husband's refusal to understand her point of view is the fault of his analyst, who is always telling him about 'le nom du père'. 'You had a mad authoritarian father,' she says, 'and now you have a mad analyst who supports you in maintaining the father's authority.'

He meanwhile knows that she chose her new analyst 'because she'll always agree with you!' He says 'Your analyst is ridiculous, she supports mollycoddling children instead of telling you how crazy you are; your analyst idealizes "*Understanding*".' The complaint of each is: you chose an analyst who will collude with you.

And in this view, each patient and analyst have – in the mind of the other – become a corrupt parental couple, or an incestuous Oedipal couple.

And the impossibility of working through the Oedipus complex goes on through generations.

In the consultations they had with me, each, unsurprisingly, wanted to pull me to their side. More: each was convinced that I would side with them, would say they are right. Convinced, then, that I would have an exclusive relationship with him or her and the other would be destroyed.

Each of two ordinary people – not monsters: adults, not children – telling me 'You are the only person who can save me, and you will, because you will see that I am right and he (or she) is wrong, and then everything will be alright.'

Each, in other words, desperate to be allowed to believe in an Oedipal illusion: that 'Mother/Father loves only me'. And each believing that only by maintaining this illusion can they be protected against the violent jealousy, envy and destructiveness of the true Oedipus situation.

It is important to understand how the identifications work and what they are for. Probably provoked by the budding sexuality of their youngest child, and their own aging, and faced with the losses inherent in these new and real events, each parent feels his own sense of security to be threatened and each reverts to a more primitive, infantile state of mind.

In this state of mind each holds himself together by means of the process Freud described so beautifully, and in a groundbreaking way, in 'Mourning and Melancholia' – that is, a concrete identification with original objects. The identifications are at multiple levels: the mother, through an identification with her child, becomes again in her mind a child faced with powerful Oedipal anxieties and fantasies. From within that identification she cannot bear what she experiences as the intolerable pain of the excluded child, and at the same time feels violent wishes to get rid of (to murder) her husband: the hated third. Behind this identification with the Oedipal child is a much earlier identification with an ideal mother (this on the model of Freud's Leonardo: she is being an ideal mother to herself as the ideal son.) From this position she forms an alliance with her child (representing her child self) to delete/destroy/murder the father. One can imagine that her own Oedipal relationship with her father was a transference of this same configuration: there are only we two.

And so she is prepared to violently change the world for this child version of herself.

The violent murderousness in the mother and son couple must play a part in provoking the violence of the father. The father himself, probably afraid of his own, long buried and never acknowledged, but still active Oedipal resentments against his own domineering father, is unable to feel sympathy for his boy – such sympathy would expose him to ancient forbidden murderous feelings of his own and, as he probably did as a child, he holds them off by an identification with his father's authority. He behaves to his son just as his father did to him: unconsciously he is his father.

Each parent unconsciously wants to enact his Oedipal desires, not to relinquish them.

'My object loves only me'. This is the ideal fantasy. 'And it is intolerable for this not to be true and real. And if it is not true and real, I want to, and am compelled to, murder my rival. Yet, at the same time, if it is true and realized, I will lose my world: I will have no mother and no father.'

This is the Oedipal dilemma; this is why the story of Oedipus is a tragedy.

You can see this play out in the material I've presented: in Mrs X's feelings that, on the one hand, it is unbearable that the child not be allowed to possess his mother – to have unimpeded access to her mind, her heart and her body – and on the other hand, a horror that this scenario means the destruction of the family.

And we can see that it also plays out in the consulting room: each wants the analyst as ally to achieve the Oedipal fantasy, not for help in understanding it. And when, as analysts, we inevitably in part go along with this fantasy – sometimes in tiny ways and sometimes, tragically, in major ones – we destroy the structure which allows our patient to grow into reality. We leave our patient without an analyst.

This Oedipal tragedy plays out again and again in our lives. We never completely outgrow the allure of the fantasy; we are always prey to its pull.

The concept of the Oedipus complex is at the core of psychoanalytic theory. Its importance lies not only in its meaning for sexual and gender identity – maybe not even primarily – but because its working through is essential for the structuring of personality. It sets in motion the evolution of a complex set of object relations: the coming into awareness of the separateness of the other person and thus the continual struggle with the awareness of there always being three objects. 'My mother and I are not one. And as soon as she is other than me, she has an-other.'

The point about the working through of the Oedipus complex is that it necessitates the recognition that the illusion – the complete possession of the ideal object – can no longer be felt to be possible. I think of this as part of what Melanie Klein called a movement from a paranoid-schizoid state of mind to a more depressive state of mind in which we give up the belief in our ideal world, suffer the pain of its loss, and, eventually, allow our objects to exist as whole people separate from ourselves.

It would be nice, I suppose, if we humans could give up, once and for all, the Oedipal illusion – the unconscious fantasy that we can live forever as part of a unity with our object. Experience shows us that such an unwavering acceptance of reality is simply not in our nature. We oscillate back and forth, again and again, between reality and a disavowal of reality: we have to rework the Oedipus situation in each new life experience, at each stage of development and each time we are faced with a threat to what we think we know. These moments threaten our view of ourselves and the world we've created in our minds; they make us anxious and helpless and arouse our hostility and we revert to a narcissistic state of mind, of concrete identifications with our objects.

So, I am arguing that we are never once and for all finished with the Oedipus complex. It is never conclusively worked through such that we are in a permanent state of the acceptance of the reality of the other person. We fight against that awareness all our lives. And then we have to struggle all over again to come to terms with it.

The idea that a complex of feelings – let alone one as powerful as the Oedipus complex – could utterly, finally, be destroyed – not remain in the unconscious, not go on existing in each of us 'as germ and fantasy' – is, it seems to me, quite un-Freudian. And it seems to me to be very Freudian to wonder why it was that Freud decided that – uniquely among human experiences – the Oedipus complex had to be abolished, demolished, dissolved.

References

Freud, S. (1910) Leonardo Da Vinci and a Memory of His Childhood. In J. Strachey (ed.), *The Standard Edition of the Complete Psychological Works of Sigmund Freud*, vol. 11 (pp. 57–138). London: Hogarth Press [1957].

Freud, S. (1917) Mourning and Melancholia. In J. Strachey (ed.), *The Standard Edition of the Complete Psychological Works of Sigmund Freud*, vol. 14 (pp. 243–258). London: Hogarth Press [1957].

Freud, S. (1924) The Dissolution of the Oedipus Complex. In J. Strachey (ed.), *The Standard Edition of the Complete Psychological Works of Sigmund Freud*, vol. 19 (pp. 171–180). London: Hogarth Press [1961].

9 On Becoming Oneself

Nabokov and The-One-Who-Isn't-Super-Pig

Priscilla Roth

Vladimir Nabokov, the great Russian émigré writer, begins his auto-biography, *Speak, Memory*, with the following description:

> In probing my childhood ... I see the awakening of consciousness as a series of spaced flashes, with the intervals between them gradually diminishing until bright blocks of perception are formed, affording memory a slippery hold. I had learned numbers and speech more or less simultaneously at a very early date, but the inner knowledge that I was I, and that my parents were my parents, seems to have been established only later, when it was directly associated with my discovering their age in relation to mine. Judging by the strong sunlight that, when I think of that revelation, immediately invades my memory with lobed sun flecks through overlapping patterns of greenery, the occasion may have been my mother's birthday, in late summer, in the country, and I had asked questions and had assessed the answers I received. All this is as it should be according to the theory of recapitulation; the beginning of reflexive consciousness in the brain of our remotest ancestor must surely have coincided with the dawning of the sense of time.
>
> Thus, when the newly disclosed, fresh and trim formula of my own age, four, was confronted with the parental formulas, thirty-three and twenty-seven, something happened to me. I was given a tremendously invigorating shock ... I felt myself plunged abruptly into a radiant and mobile medium that was none other than the pure element of time. One shared it ... with creatures that were not oneself but that were joined to one by time's common flow ... At that instant, I became acutely aware that the twenty-seven-year-old being, in soft white and pink, holding my left hand, was my mother, and the thirty-three-year-old being, in hard white and gold, holding my right hand, was my father. Between them, as they evenly progressed, I strutted.
>
> (Nabokov, 1989, p. 1)

So, linked to both his parents and at the same time suddenly aware of difference – in age, in generation, in gender, in time from one moment to

DOI: 10.4324/9781003588870-12

another – reflexive consciousness came to the four year old Nabokov. Consciousness, perception, them in relation to me – life 'shared with creatures that were not oneself but were joined to one'.

I'll come back to Nabokov later.

Any worthwhile exploration of the question of identity has to consider at least the philosophical, the political, the cultural as well as the psychological aspects of the issue: the question of identity is multi-faceted and enormously complex. As a psychoanalyst, I am interested in what happens within the psychological development of an individual to enable him to form an authentic self, a sense that 'I am I'; and the converse, what may be some interferences to such a development.

I want to begin tonight by re-stating two familiar formulations, the first from psychoanalysis, and the second more generally philosophical. The first is the notion, fundamental to contemporary psychoanalytic thinking, that the early ego forms itself around its experiences of a good object. At the beginning of life the individual ego (the sort of pre-self) is weak, unintegrated, dispersed and incoherent. The building up of the ego from which evolves a sense of self with the capacity for self-reflection, depends on its experiences of itself in its repeated experiences with a good other, whom it is constitutionally prepared to expect and recognize and which it can, as it were, take into itself and with whom it can identify. Thus, during the first months of life the self is integrated by gathering together experiences which at the first are unconnected, because there is no memory yet, and uniting them with the good object. The ego thus passes from complete dispersion and discontinuity, to the cohesion brought about by experiences of gratification with a recognizable other. Another way of putting that is to say that the question, 'Who am I?' begins to be answered from very early on in our lives, as we take in, identify with and react to our primary loved objects. Here I've just been repeating in psychoanalytic terms what Nabokov conveyed so vividly.

My second assumption is a more philosophical one. It is the idea that our sense of identity rests in our not having to ask the question, 'Who am I?'. That when I feel I know who I am, the question 'Who am I?' doesn't arise to be answered: I take for granted that I am me, and that if I couldn't say exactly what that means, I am at least comfortable that it means something with some solidity. My ability to carry on in the world depends on this. It is what philosophers call 'ontological security'. In psychoanalytic terms, it corresponds to a feeling that one's internal world is peopled by figures who are, for the most part, at peace with each other and with oneself.

But this sense of who we are – our identity – is at one and the same time both sturdy and fragile. Most people, most of the time, take it for granted: it is relied upon and unquestioned. But each of us is aware that the moment it is questioned – the moment it really comes into question- we are apt to find that just on the other side of the membrane that surrounds the coherence of our Ego – our sense of 'I am me' – lies chaos. It is a chaos marked by the sense that I am 'nothing'; there is no real essential Me.

Psychoanalysts describe this chaos as dis-integration; a feeling of falling to pieces. At such times meaning, which was taken for granted, disappears, links which mattered and had strength have no strength. Most of us have had at least some brief experience of such terrifying states of mind, mildly or severely, awake or in our dreams. It is about losing our sense of the stability of our self-identity, about organization and structure dissolving. And because our view of our self is intimately bound up with our view of our internal objects and their view of us, what we experience is a collapse of our inner world. (We protect ourselves, when we can, against such awful dissolution, sometimes by creating false structures when we cannot rely on real ones.)

I am going briefly to discuss current psychoanalytic concepts of how a sense of identity is formed and how it is linked with the process of identification. I will then describe one way in which this process can become de-railed, and become a means not of establishing one's own identity – a mind of one's own – but of taking on and over the personality of someone else. I will then tell you about a little boy who seems to have had to answer the terrifying question, 'Who am I?' by insisting 'I am him'.

In the development of psychoanalytic theory, the question of identity has always been linked to that of identification. In 'Mourning and Melancholia' (1917), Freud famously described the way in which the loss of the object becomes an identification with the object. I say famously to emphasize how fundamental the formulations he spelt out in that paper are to all later psycho-analytic thinking about who one is, and how personality is formed. In order to understand this, it is necessary to emphasize what he meant – and what psy-choanalysts mean by 'loss of the object'. It is a concept which is easily mis-understood, because it appears to be so easily understandable. At the risk of telling you what you already know, and for the sake of being absolutely clear, I want to discuss it for a moment. The object is experienced as lost not because it has died, or gone away, or been unfaithful, although any of these conditions may be part of the experience. I lose my object when there is a discontinuity in my sense of it and relationship to it; my knowledge of it; my (of course illusory) conviction that it is exactly as I imagine or make it to be, and thus entirely and completely limited by my conception of it. I'll give an example. During a session with a woman patient a number of years ago, in the middle of an interpretation, the telephone ran and continued to ring. The phone was on the other side of the room, and when it didn't stop after two or three rings I apologized to the patient and got up from my chair, answered the phone, told the caller I couldn't speak at that moment, returned to my chair and, after a moment, continued my inter-pretation. The patient was silent for a minute, and then, in a tone filled with a kind of terror and awe said, 'When you got up from your chair, it was a shock: as if my arm had simply got up off my body and walked across the room'. What she was conveying was the power of her belief that I am a personification of her fantasies of me; I can only do and be what she fantasizes me to be able to do. She no more imagined I could get up off my chair in the middle of the session, than that her arm could, of its own accord, separate itself from her body.

Such experiences require a re-jigging of our sense of ourselves in relation to others – a recognition of separateness and of the real existence and independence of others, and of the tiny and immense ways we all have of denying and disbelieving this. When, using all our subtle capacities for self-delusion, we unconsciously believe our objects are limited by our fantasies of them, when we can't distinguish the external world from our internals worlds, we are, unconsciously of course, treating other people as though they were parts or extensions of ourselves, as though they and we were one.

What Freud realized, and brilliantly described in 'Mourning and Melancholia', is that when this experience of loss is experienced as the loss of a part of the self, then knowing about the loss, actually experiencing it as a loss, is powerfully resisted; in fact, it is rejected. Instead, a part of the self (a part of the ego) identifies with the lost object, and becomes like it – the object is thus incorporated into a part of the self, and the potentially catastrophic feeling of object loss is denied. 'I have not lost it, I *am* it'. Or, as Freud put it better, 'The shadow of the object falls upon the ego'. Why shadow? Because Freud understood that the object is hated for its separateness, its uncontrollability and its independence, and hated because its capacity to come and go threatens the subject's omnipotence. So that melancholia – depression – which feels like the self being attacked from inside – came to be understood as one part of the melancholic's self attacking another part which is actually felt to be the object, now installed in the ego and experienced as part of the self. (If all this seems complicated, or too theoretical, you will understand what I mean if you think about the times you've thought about someone: 'God, she's becoming just like her mother'. This is rarely meant as a compliment.)

Six years later, in 'The Ego and the Id' (1923), Freud extended this idea of identification way beyond melancholia – he had come to understand that identifications – the installation inside a part of the ego – of aspects of other people, take place each time an object relationship has to be given up. Again, this means not actually the loss of the object as an external figure, but the loss of the version of the object that the subject has organized in his own mind. The classical and earliest case is weaning: weaning is an enormous loss for the baby, even when it doesn't involve a loss of his actual mother or her time or concern – it is a loss of his illusion that the breast is his, belongs to him, will always be his. It is the loss of this illusion that he has to deal with, and how he deals with it – including, of course, what help he gets from his mother to deal with it – will determine his ability to deal with later losses.

So, to simplify: if who he thinks he is infant and breast, and he cannot accommodate, cannot stand the pain of suddenly not being that, but having instead to be just-plain-old-infant relating to someone else who is the breast; if he cannot bear the loss of that illusory identity, he may cling to the illusion by incorporating (in phantasy, but in his unconscious in reality) the breast with its desirable and, as well, hated aspects – he may, in his mind identify with a particular version of this breast – he doesn't lose it, he becomes it.

Now it is very important to differentiate partial identifications which take place in all of us in relation to all our important objects, from those identifications which are global and feel complete and total, as if the Other has been swallowed whole. The first, more normal identifications, are multiple and varied and allow for a flexibility of the object within the personality – one could say it is about an identification which at the same time acknowledges the non-me-ness of the object: I am like my mother. I am not my mother. In the second, more pathological kind of identification, the whole object is devoured and taken over and at the same time takes over the personality. The 'rump'-ego is submerged and weakened – only that part of the ego which has swallowed up and become swollen with the incorporated object is visible, loud and obvious. The person seeming to be a caricature of the object he has swallowed up. People who walk around as though they think they are the Good Breast don't really seem like an ordinary, run-of-the-mill Good Breast – they seem like a horrible parody of the notion of a good breast: that is, the good breast viewed with envy and hatred. It is this distorted image of the envied object which is so powerfully introjected (taken in) and identified with, and is one reason why the massive introjective identification immediately feels 'off' to the observer. It always includes smugness, even when the smugness includes a smug self-depreciation.

So, when this process is massive and seemingly all-consuming, when his own personality seems to be submerged in the swallowed up personality of the other (so that, as Abraham beautifully put it, now the 'Bright radiance of the object shines upon the ego'), he is in a state of a particular kind of confusion of identities, a particular form of projective identification – described by Ignês Sodré (2004) as 'massive pathological introjective identification'. (I am stressing that I agree with Ignês Sodré and others that it makes sense to refer to this process as introjective because I think we need to dis-assemble the projection-is-bad, introjection-is-good dichotomy; and because I think the experience of being occupied by and merged with a devoured and consumed object has qualities peculiar to that process which needs to be examined.)

Melanie Klein's development of the concept of the depressive position enabled us to better understand the building up of an internal world, from the earliest part-object introjections to a highly complex inner world with relationships between the self and its objects and between the internal objects themselves. She spoke of the introjection, the taking inside oneself of objects so that they are felt to be established inside the self as good, loving and supportive: in me but not me. A good example is the super-ego: the conscience, which feels like an object inside, with whom the ego is sometimes at peace, sometimes in conflict.

The pathologically introjected object is an object into whom massive projections have occurred. But, introjecting it in such a way that it takes over as if it were the self, has serious consequences for the personality of the subject: he feels he has objects inside him who are in a terrible state. This is partly because at the same time that he has massively identified with and taken over the object – by being it – the object has also been introjected and remains as a separate internal object, and in its separate state it is felt to be weak and suffering, and therefore it makes him guilty and persecuted. In addition, the subject loses his own personality, which becomes either weak and enfeebled, or entirely projected; his effective personality becomes rigid and brittle.

We understand a feeling of well-being, of inner resilience, to be dependent on an inner world peopled by objects felt to be alive and able to relate freely to the self and to other objects. In contrast, this state of massive introjective identification is a state of apparent smugness masking emptiness, deadness and imminent chaos. So, what I am describing is a situation in which an experience of the loss of the object is felt to be so catastrophically dangerous to the identity of the self, that the person protects himself from the danger of falling to pieces by incorporating and imprisoning the object within his personality. The question 'Who am I?' can thus be (unconsciously) answered 'I am him'.

Justin

Justin is a seven-year-old boy who turned up in a large child guidance clinic in a city in the United States. I have had the opportunity of supervising his therapy on a number of occasions, and I am grateful to his therapist for allowing me to use his material to illustrate the process I have been describing.

As I said, Justin is seven, although when his therapist first described him to me she said 'He's seven … going on forty-seven'. She described him as one of those awful children who irritates everybody. What was annoying and unpleasant about him was his impenetrable smugness – in a seven-year-old, remember – his superiority and arrogance, his capacity to make others, even grown-ups, feel put down by him. He never played; he taught or demonstrated. He didn't read books; he wrote books. He would carefully, oh-so-carefully, teach his therapist to colour something in the way he had coloured it, or repeat the lines of a simple poem she was to learn by heart, and then would praise her with the excruciatingly empty, 'Well, I think that's very good'. When he didn't like something that was going on he would pull over an adult and confide, 'Look, I'm afraid I'm not feeling very comfortable with this situation'.

(All children play at this sometimes. All children want a go at being teacher, or boss, or father. The thing about Justin was, he was like that all the time – as far as one could see, that was Justin.) Phony, priggish, he put people off. (Mock baby-ness – quite repugnant as well, sulky and pouty.)

Justin was brought to the clinic by his parents, not because of his difficult and unlikeable personality, but because, although he was perfect in most ways, unfortunately he also frequently soiled himself. So, there was this awful strange juxtaposition of the middle-aged arrogant little boy, reeking of his own mess. His mother, a depressed and tired youngish woman, seemed concerned and worried about him – she is a registered nurse who was frequently required to be on night duty, and therefore much of Justin's daily care had been left to his father. His father was an older man who, when psychotherapy was suggested for his son, replied, 'Oh, that's fine, I know everything about psychotherapy'. In fact, he is disdainful of the therapy and treats Justin with ill-disguised annoyance, mixed with occasional signs of genuinely puzzled distress, punctuated by 'interpretations' of Justin's psychopathology. Father also occasionally offers interpretations of mother's psychopathology.

In the early months Justin's sessions were always the same. He ignored his therapist when she went to get him from the waiting room – he got up immediately and walked to the therapy room, but it was as though she was not there, as though he just owned the place. Inside the room he would only, and relentlessly do what he knew – he would make clever paper constructions, often cutting out and constructing paper houses, or many sided boxes. What he powerfully conveyed was that he didn't need any help from anybody. Not only did he not seem to think it would be there, he didn't expect it or look for it – he didn't seem to have ever considered the question 'Can this person help me?' Instead, as the months went by, his play in the session gradually began to illuminate his mental structure.

I'd like to tell you about one particular session. It followed several months of really repetitive play in which he made things he knew how to make and gave his therapist lectures on various subjects. But one day, something else happened. He suddenly took two little plastic pink pigs from his toy box and began to play out a story with them. He called the pigs 'Super-Pig' and 'The-One-Who-Isn't-Super-Pig'.

Talking in the squeaky voices of the pigs, he said 'let's go to sleep'. He decided to give them a bath before they went to bed, so he filled a small toy container and soaked the pigs in it, scrubbing them and then carefully drying them. Then he put them to sleep inside the house.

He went over and filled the sink in the room with water, then walked back to check on the sleeping pigs. In a suddenly harsh voice, he went on with the story: 'While they sleep the dam gets polluted!' He rushed over to the sink holding the paint palette, wet the paint brush in the sink and violently stabbed the paint palette several times, then trailed the dirty brush in the sink. He repeated this several times, penetrating the water with red, brown, orange and black paint. The water looked disgusting. Justin seemed pleased.

He got the small container that he had used to bathe the pigs before they went to bed and tied a little bit of string to it, making the other end of the string hang into the dirty water in the sink. In a matter-of-fact tone he said that while the pigs slept the water passed through the pipes from the polluted dam and filled up their bath. He said 'the disgusting, polluted water comes into the pigs' bath!' He added that the weird thing was that 'during the night the pigs had a strange dream that all the water had got polluted, and when they woke up, they discovered it was all true'. He repeated emphatically that what they dreamed was really true.

The therapist understood that Justin was showing her something important. She said to him how frightening it feels to him that he can't tell the difference between what happens in his mind – his phantasies and thoughts – from what really happens in the world. She said that when he imagines or dreams that everything is polluted and dirty and impossibly mucked up, he feels everything really is like that, inside him and outside him.

He looked at her and nodded. Then he went on narrating the 'story', as though she weren't there.

'When the pigs wake up', Justin said, 'The-One-Who-Isn't-Super-Pig wants to have a bath, and he climbs into the bath, but it's filthy and dirty, and he doesn't know what to do, and has to be rescued from it by Super-Pig.' Super-Pig takes over: he decided to build a fence around the big dam, the really polluted dam, and he issues instructions to The-One-Who-Isn't-Super-Pig, to go get bits of plastic fencing to put around the sink which is the dam. The-One-Who-Isn't-Super-Pig does this, but it turns out there are in fact (that is, in the actual toy box in the therapy room) not enough plastic fences to go round the whole sink. Now Justin gets worried, and anxious, and frantically begins cutting up bits of paper to fill the gaps.

There is a brief moment where it looks like they've triumphed, and Justin even decides that it's perfectly safe for the two pigs to frolic about in the polluted water for a little while: 'They're impervious to the poison', he says. But then suddenly this doesn't seem to work, because The-One-Who-Isn't-Super-Pig fell all the way in and screamed 'Help! Yuk', and seemed really to be drowning in the muck. Super-Pig came to his rescue, pulled him out, and saved his life. Then, said Justin, the two pigs went home in Super-Pig's car; adding, 'The-One-Who-Isn't-Super-Pig doesn't have his own house or car. Super-Pig just lets him borrow his.'

I'll stop the material here for the moment and take a look at what it shows us. I don't think it's difficult to see that this new play of Justin's shows important things about what is going on inside him, and how his personality has become structured, and, I think, illustrates some of the points I have been making.

What we can see is that Justin is walking around as Super-Pig. Super-Pig has lots of qualities, but the main ones are that he is super – he can do everything – and that he's a pig – which I think means he can have everything. When Justin ignores his therapist when she comes to get him, when he walks through the corridor and into the room 'as though he owns the place', it is Justin as Super-Pig – in his mind he does own the place. He doesn't read books, remember – he writes books. He is the possessor of all knowledge and all power. As he says, Super-Pig owns the house and the car: he is it all, and has it all, and knows it all.

As Super-Pig he is protected from being polluted by doubt or anxiety or guilt or shame. But because he has all the expertise nobody else is felt to be able to have anything to give him or any way of being able to help him. Not that, as Super-Pig, he needs help.

And then there is The-One-Who-Isn't-Super-Pig. The-One-Who-Isn't-Super-Pig is who Justin would be if he couldn't be Super-Pig. And The-One-Who-Isn't-Super-Pig doesn't have anything – not a house, not a car, not the ability to save himself – not even an identity: he's just the one who isn't something.

Karl Abraham – who was, by the way, Melanie Klein's analyst – wrote in his 1924 paper about a patient of his, a man who constantly berated himself for being lazy and worthless. His picture of his parents was that his father was lazy and worthless, and his mother was constantly critical of him. This patient felt himself to be 'just like' his father, but what Abraham was able to see and to show him was, naturally enough, that that wasn't the whole story: he was, in fact, 'just like' both his parents: a part of him identified with his mother, and was constantly berating a part of him identified with his father. In other words, this patient contained within himself (and therefore could control) both parents by being both of them engaged in a cruel relationship scripted by him in his mind.

Similarly: I think Justin felt he could not cope with his awful feelings of smallness, which made him believe himself to be incapable of saving his parents from his attacks on them inside himself. I think he felt that everything had been polluted and destroyed, outside but also inside him, in his feelings, so that in his inner world there were no loving parents and no loved Justin. And so he dealt with his hopelessness by magical means: it is as if he had swallowed up a bloated father/mother imago, and by swallowing it he had made it his, and gets to be it. It is a strange and horrible imago (a 'combined object') – it has qualities of both his actual parents – their superior knowl-edge, their sexuality, their capacity to survive in the world, but these are caricatured and bloated beyond recognition by his projections into them and by his envy and jealousy of them.

I want to look more closely at the material, but first I want to suggest that when Justin first appears he is not likeable – he is false. When, later, Justin shows us something of what he is struggling with, when we can integrate in our own minds Justin as Super-Pig and Justin as The-One-Who-Isn't-Super-Pig, as well as Justin struggling with all this, he is very likeable indeed. This struggle to sort out and to integrate difficult and incongruous facets of our personality is the human struggle to determine our authentic identity.

To return to the material which I'd like to look at more closely: Justin tries to clean the pigs before they go to sleep, so their sleep will be all right, so that the dirt of the day, the bad feelings, are washed away. The pigs are clean.

But while the pigs (who represent Justin) sleep, terrible things happen: the play with the paint and paintbrush in the sink, the pollution which mucks up the sink and gets back into the little pigs' bath, immediately brings to mind Justin's soiling. Everything is being polluted, he says, everyone is in terrible danger. But I want to suggest that the play tells us something more: that it tells us about Justin's view of what his parents do while he's sleeping (while the little pigs sleep), and the way this picture of them connects with his soiling. I think the play with the paintbrush and paint is not just about something being soiled and polluted, it is a depiction of a terrible phantasy he has about what his parents are doing when he is alone all by himself in his bed, when his jealousy and hatred of his parents being together at night, and the violent feelings this arouses in him, colour his perception of their relationship, their intercourse. Justin imagines his father violently attacking his mother (like the brush stabbing violently at the palette) and imagines that she becomes filthy and disgusting as a result. He emphasizes to his therapist that this goes on inside him – in his thoughts and in his dreams – and outside him too. I think this a beautiful description and illustration of the powerful effects of projection and introjection. Having to be alone, and leave them to their private sexual relationship, creates violent, turbulent feelings in him; these feelings colour and powerfully affect how he imagines their relationship. Furthermore, when he thinks of their relationship as violent and disgusting, he takes that picture back into his mind – and inside him, filling his dreams and thoughts is a filthy and disgusting sexual couple. You will remember that there is only one pipe that leads to and from the bath and the polluted dam – the filth goes back and forth, with no other way out. He feels violently about his parents, he projects his violence into them and views them violently, he is then filled with violent feelings.

These phantasies, which deeply trouble him, express themselves in his most disturbingly obvious symptom, his encopresis, soiling himself. Like all symptoms, this one is over-determined; it doesn't mean just one thing, it has a variety of different meanings. In the first place, I think his faeces probably represent to him his idealized but actually useless internal object: at some level he holds on to a belief that it is fabulous and precious; at another level he knows it is just shit. Secondly, I think he believes his faeces are the babies he can produce in his own tummy, in rivalry with his parents. Thirdly, it is shit masquerading as jewels, and as the producer of this, Justin is identified with a self-idealizing object who grossly over-values his own productions: his thoughts or wisdom or words. Justin's soiling is also, of course, an attack on his parents, and as such is his biggest source of shame and guilt. It is in his mind a polluting of his parents and their relationship and their love for him. He feels deeply ashamed and guilty about this, and hopeless about being able to clean up the mess. And he is stuck in a system in which things just go back and forth: he pollutes them, they pollute him. And of course soiling is about his feeling a mess and not being in control of anything inside him – it's all smelly and awful, and just oozes out.

Only by being Super-Pig can he pretend to be safe. Super-Pig has the car and the house: Super-Pig can be Father and Mother – and in this way doesn't have to be jealous or left out or get stuck in mucky feelings. Super-Pig is impervious to the poison – to the painful, disorganizing experience of being a little boy alone and very vulnerable.

But Justin doesn't completely become Super-Pig. Notice how protective, as Super-Pig, he is of The-One-Who-Isn't-Super-Pig: how he brings it along with him, like a nearly useless part of him, terribly enfeebled, but also precious and not expendable or completely destroyed. The-One-Who-Isn't-Super-Pig represents what is left of Justin's own real self: weak, and with few resources, but still around and needing to be looked after and able to ask for help.

So: in this session Justin is showing his therapist how he is nearly completely identified with an all-powerful object (father or father/mother combined in some phantastic way). But the very fact that he can show this to her, and plays it out with and for her, shifts things inside him. Justin begins to use his therapy to help him to work things out.

A session some weeks later, from which I'll just tell you a fragment, illustrates how the process, which began with the Super-Pig material, developed. In this session, he left the two pigs in the box, and instead took all of the furniture from the house and tried to build an enormous tower on top of which he wanted to stand the little boy doll. The little boy doll, he said, needed to get to the top of the tower in order to get to the moon.

Using the toy furniture, he focused his attention on building as high a tower as possible. In each attempt he tried to add more furniture: chairs, baths, cupboards, tables; there was no logic, thought or planning involved in this, and each time the tower tumbled down, he would start again, equally illogically. This went on for a frustratingly long time.

Eventually he managed to make some part of it stay up, though it was only half as high as he wanted, and it was not high enough to go to the moon. He resorted to fetching a small toy cannon, holding this on top of the smallish tower, and shooting the little boy up to the moon. The moon was high up (the little boy doll was clinging to a ledge high up on the wall), and now the little boy doll became afraid of falling – he couldn't get down! Justin scrambled in his box again, and, sorting through the animals, took out two crocodiles: he said there were 'the good croc' and 'the bad croc', and they would help the little boy get down. The good croc got the bad croc to help save the little boy's life: he couldn't do it alone. They did it by pushing down the tower to get the boy down. When the therapist commented on the bad croc helping, Justin smirked, and said, 'He only helps because he likes pushing down towers, certainly not to be nice.'

The session ended with the little boy on a ship in the sink; the ship circling round and round in a sad desultory way, as if not much was happening.

I think this session shows us the next stage in Justin's working through of his problem. He is no longer Super-Pig; he has, to some extent at least, begun to loosen the identification with the powerful object. He's now a little boy, trying pretty desperately to keep up his spirits, trying to be very high up and not left in the muck. But he can't really build a proper tower, he can't use his mind to think and figure out how to do it, because his mind is in disconnected, disorganized pieces, which don't fit together. This is terribly interesting and important to think about: Justin is potentially a bright child.

There is no reason why he shouldn't be able to build the tower in a rational way: larger things on the bottom, smaller towards the top, and so on. And in fact, I would assume that when he was Super-Pig he could easily have built the tower properly. But at this moment, when the Super-Pig identification is being given up, he is 'worse off' than he was before: he has lost the structure he relied on, and his mind has fallen into a much more disorganized state.

But unlike in the Super-Pig material, where there were no helpful others at all – in this material Justin knows that the little boy needs help to come down from the tower. He knows that being that high up is dangerous, that he's got to get down and that he needs help to do so. He is beginning to recognize that his therapist is helping him, and that he needs her help to come down from this dangerously high place he gets into.

But he also lets her know that he thinks he cannot trust her, even when she does help him – 'He only does it because he likes knocking down towers', Justin says of the bad croc who helps the little boy down, 'certainly not because he's nice'.

I think this is a development that brings its own problems with it. When Justin is a Super-Pig, he is in a pathological identification with the as-if-perfect object – he is the object. As such he is unhelpful, partly because, since he contains everything (the house and the car) his real objects have been left emptied of anything that might help.

But once this identification begins to loosen, once there are real objects in the external world with the potential capacity to help him, Justin is threatened with having to be dependent on them. The material shows how he then feels them to be untrustworthy. He needs his therapist to help sort things out, but he can't believe that she doesn't do it to triumph over him, just because she 'likes knocking down towers', which I think means likes feeling better than him, knocking him down. (How much this is characteristic of his real objects – his actual parents – we don't know. His father, particularly, may contribute to this view of someone who only wants to help in order to make himself feel big and powerful.) What we do know is that Justin himself, in his smug Super-Pig state, can pretend to be helpful while actually triumphing over the other person; remember how he would teach the therapist to do something and then praise her in a phony, smarmy way. And it is this destructive triumph that he now expects from her.

Justin's problem is that when he stays on top of the tower he is unreachable; when he begins to be able to be reached, he becomes paranoid about his objects: 'They don't do it to help me, they do it to triumph over me. They pretend to be good, but they are really bad.'

Of course this isn't the whole story: as well as the bad croc, there is the good croc – Justin's fear now is that his trust in his good object isn't strong enough to withstand his distrust of it. Working through this became the next challenge in his therapy. But what is obvious is that the rigidity, the fixed, repetitive quality of the massive introjective identification, which marked those long early months of therapy, had begun to alter and change. We can see so much movement in this material, so much more of a relationship to people. His imagination is freer; he is much les imprisoned in a fixed, tight hold on a useless, deadened identification. For all his continuing difficulties, Justin is becoming himself.

I am getting to the end of what I want to say, but first I want to suggest that what I have been talking about might be a way of thinking about a difference between remembering and repeating (Freud). Justin as Super-Pig endlessly repeats inside himself his earliest relationships – he doesn't recognize their movement or the loss of them.

Remembering, on the other hand, may be about a relationship with live, unbiddable internal objects – unbiddable because we are only occasionally, when we're lucky, able to have a conscious emotional sense of them – we cannot be them. Nabokov (1989) looks at a moon over a winter road in New England and conjures up the 'lusty frosts' of the Russia of his lost childhood. This is about being in contact with memories and experiences of people and places which are at the same time palpably experienced as lost. It is about having to know how unbiddable, how untrappable, these emotional experiences and memories are; like the emotions about them, they cannot be deliberately evoked; they cannot be forced into being. They are in sharp contrast to the lumpen, dead quality of internal objects who have been made one's own – trapped forever in the rigidity of one's control of them.

Nabokov writes that from his mother, who treasured her capacity to remember, he inherited 'the beauty of intangible property, unreal estate' … which was 'splendid training for the endurance of later losses' (Nabokov, 1989, p. 40).

His memories of her are specific: on a particular day she did a particular thing, but also his specific memories of her become as if repetitive, habitual ones – so typical of the way childhood is experienced, so that: 'She *would lay out* the mushrooms in concentric circles … her face *would show* an odd, cheerless expression … she *would stand there* admiring them' (Nabokov, 1989, p. 44; my emphasis). I think this is the grown-up Nabokov's way of extending and stretching experience, in order to keep memory not as a capricious, momentary event but as part of an enduring picture of his loved object in his mind.

This is a man who lost his childhood home, his country – he is an exile and everything he once knew has gone – his father was murdered, his mother died in poverty. He has no concrete reminders of the past … he is, in fact, remembering in order to rescue them all from oblivion:

> I see again my schoolroom in Vyra, the blue roses of the wallpaper, the open window. Its reflection fills the oval mirror above the leathern couch where my uncle sits, gloating over a tattered book. A sense of security, of well being, of summer warmth pervades my memory. That robust reality makes a ghost of the present. The mirror brims with brightness; a bumblebee has entered the room and bumps against the ceiling. Everything is at it should be, nothing will ever change, nobody will ever die.
>
> (Nabokov, 1989, p. 77)

But of course, the man who writes these words knows, and knows that we know, that in fact everything changes, and everyone dies.

As these images appear in his mind, his internal objects (his lost loved ones) are re-vitalized – they come back to him from, and I quote him to finish, 'those distant times whose long light finds so many ingenious ways to reach me' (Nabokov, 1989, p. 118).

References

Abraham, K. (1924) A Short Study of the Development of the Libido Viewed in the Light of Mental Disorders. In K. Abraham, *Selected Papers on Psychoanalysis*. London: Routledge [1988].

Freud, S. (1914) Remembering, Repeating and Working-Through (Further Recommendations on the Technique of Psycho-Analysis II). In J. Strachey (ed.), *The Standard Edition of the Complete Psychological Works of Sigmund Freud*, vol. 12 (pp. 145–156). London: Hogarth Press [1958].

Freud, S. (1917) Mourning and Melancholia. In J. Strachey (ed.), *The Standard Edition of the Complete Psychological Works of Sigmund Freud*, vol. 14 (pp. 243–258). London: Hogarth Press [1957].

Freud, S. (1923) The Ego and The Id. In J. Strachey (ed.), *The Standard Edition of the Complete Psychological Works of Sigmund Freud*, vol. 19. London: Hogarth Press [1961].

Nabokov, V. (1989) *Speak, Memory: An Autobiography Revisited*. New York: Knopf Doubleday Publishing Group.

Sodré, I. (2004) 'Who's Who': Notes on pathological Identifications' In Pursuit of Psychic Change: ed. Hargreaves, E. and Varchevker, A. Also in I. Sodré (2015) Imaginary Existences: A psychoanalytic exploration of phantasy, fiction, dreams and daydreams: (The New Library of Psychoanalysis), ed. Roth, P., London: Routledge.

10 Melanie Klein on Envy

Priscilla Roth

This chapter is an exploration of Melanie Klein's 'Envy and Gratitude', and a testament to its fruitfulness and complexity. Written just a few years before the end of Klein's life, the elaboration of her mature views on love and hatred marked a culmination of her previous work and a radical addition to it.

Klein's conviction is that all psychological development evolves from the experience and the internalization of the first relationship to the mother:

> Throughout my work I have attributed fundamental importance to the infant's first object relation – the relationship to the mother's breast and to the mother – and have drawn the conclusion that if this primal object, which is introjected, takes root in the ego with relative security, the basis for a satisfactory development is laid. Innate factors contribute to this bond.
>
> (Klein, 1957, p. 3)

Everything that follows in her book reflects this conviction. It is impossible properly to understand Klein's discussion of the destructive power of envy separate from her belief that its perniciousness lies precisely in its fundamental interference with the establishment of the loved and loving good object within the ego – 'the foundation for hope, trust, and belief in goodness'. She believed that an expectation of this 'inexhaustible' breast was inborn and that it soon begins to stand for life and for creativity. She also believed, following Freud, that the early months of life were characterized by the struggle between the life instinct – represented by love for breast and mother – and the death instinct, represented by envy of the breast's 'intolerable goodness'.

The book was immediately surrounded by controversy, focused on what was seen to be Klein's insistence on the constitutionality of envy and its relation to the death instinct. In fact, Klein is clear that 'the capacity for both love and for destructive impulses is, *to some extent*, constitutional, though varying individually in strength and *interacting from the beginning with external conditions*' (Klein, 1957, p. 180; my emphasis). However, the juxtaposition of the power of the relationship to the breast with the deadly destructiveness of an innate hatred of the very goodness of the breast sent a

DOI: 10.4324/9781003588870-13

shudder through the British psychoanalytic community, presenting to some readers a drama of stark contrasts, easily reduced to a battle between good and evil. In fact, the issues are far more complicated and multi-dimensional and, in spite of the controversy, continue to engender important developments in psychoanalytic understanding and to be of enormous clinical value.

The question of when envy first emerges is not insignificant. Klein's view that it is 'operative from birth' has theoretical consequences: primary envy is so singularly pernicious, its effects so far reaching, because it prevents bi-polar splitting, the infant's first and essential defence. The argument goes like this: In order for the infant to deal with both powerful internal conflicts and the frustrations and demands of external reality, its ego must gradually strengthen and develop. Random sensations, perceptions and impulses must little by little become structured and comprehensible – this requires an ego of some strength and cohesion. The first task for the infant, then, is the organization and structuring of its ego and the organization of its experience so that it can begin, more or less accurately, to perceive and manage internal and external events. Capable of perceiving and responding to objects from the beginning of life, the infant is also capable from the beginning of experiencing events and objects felt to be attached to them, as good (e.g. a warm full tummy) or bad (hunger pains, colic). The infant begins internalizing, incorporating, identifying with good experiences from the first: they 'take root in his ego', and gradually his ego coheres around these repeated, eventually expectable, experiences of his good object. In other words, he gradually begins to have an unconscious sense of himself, largely based on and dependent upon his sense of his good object in good experiences. Binary splitting allows the infant to protect his sense of his good object, on which his growing sense of himself is based, from his own feelings of hatred and rage – his innate hatred as well as the rage growing out of inevitable frustrations – thereby safeguarding his mind to allow it to develop and strengthen. If envious feelings during those earliest weeks prevent the good breast from being experienced as good (ideal), its introjection is impeded. Since it is the identification with an internalized good (ideal) object that leads to a strengthening of the ego, enabling it to begin to cope with increasing increments of reality, an interference by primary envy with this identification has profound effects on all future development.

There is, however, a problem with this argument. The infant, in Klein's view, splits the world not only into Good and Bad, but, simultaneously, into Me and Not-Me, and these splits overlap: Me is felt to be everything good, including the good object; everything bad (bad self/bad object) is felt to be Not-Me. This being so, during the period when an infant's experience is one of unity with his ideal object – whether this is primary or secondary (defensive) – the ideal object is experienced as Me. The question then is how can the breast be 'intolerably good' if it is experienced as Me? How can envy interfere at this stage? I think one can conceptualize this if one thinks of mini-moments of awareness of a gap from the beginning. But if we were to think of envy as powerful enough to prevent any internalization and identification with the good (ideal) object at this early stage, we would need to imagine not only a particularly strong quantum of envy, but an underdevelopment of the infant's primary defensive organization: his ability to protect himself from the invasiveness of the world, in the most fundamental, life serving way: his ability to feel he and his good object are one.

Unity, Narcissism, Separateness

Experiences of envy and experiences of gratitude depend on an awareness of separateness – an awareness of the otherness of the other. It is hard to formulate a concept of envy which could take place within a relationship of absolute fusion between self and object; as long as what is 'Good' is experienced as 'Me', (part of me, an extension of Me) what is experienced as good need *never* be envied, since it belongs to me. Similarly, gratitude can only be experienced in relation to another person a 'Not-Me.' Klein believed that momentary awareness of the actual separateness of the object begins from birth. She believed that infants have an inborn awareness of a separate, bountiful object – a pre-conception in Bion's (1962) terms – which is met at the first feeding experience by the reality of the breast.

The goodness of the breast is not in the first instance to do with its actual qualities, it is to do with the infant's projection into it of an ideal munificence. It is the arrival of what has been expected. However much the propensity for envy or the capacity for gratitude may be constitutional – may be manifestations of the life and death instincts – and Klein certainly believes they are – *experientially* these emotions cannot exist in their true form until there has been some, at least momentary, awareness of separateness, whether this arrives, as Klein obviously thought, at or just after birth, or whether such momentary awareness arrives some weeks later. Issues of separateness, then, are fundamental to the exploration of the concepts of envy and gratitude.

But one of the corollaries of Klein's view that at the beginning the infant's perceptions of his world are split into Good = Me and Bad = Not-Me is that splitting exists as a vital defence mechanism from the beginning of life. It is the splitting of the object into 'Good' and 'bad' which protects the baby from 'the invasiveness of the world' before he is equipped to deal with it. Splitting at this very early stage is a biological necessity, protecting the infant's ability to feel he and his good object are one.

From a Kleinian point of view, the experience of pain, distress, discomfort exists in the earliest life of every baby; the infant's capacity to split his experiences into 'Good Me', 'Bad Not-Me' constitute his capacity to protect his vital relationships with his good object. Thus, the existence of a Bad Not-Me object is completely necessary. This is different from theories where there is a beginning in which it impossible to have no awareness of Bad. It is a way of thinking about an early infancy in which there is both the possibility of envy and a recognition of bad experiences.

What distinguishes Klein's theory is her insistence that primary, immediate binary splitting is essential for the possibility of life.

Klein (1957) emphasized that envious and hateful impulses are frequently split off from the patient's awareness, and that re-introducing them to the patient requires great sensitivity and care and 'only becomes possible after long and painstaking work' (p. 221).

Thus, issues of separateness – about narcissistic organizations and how they operate, or a capacity to allow a differentiation between self and object – have become of increasing interest among Kleinian and increasingly frequently also non-Kleinian writers. At the same time there is a growing sense of the complexity and interweaving of concepts, so that an examination of envy leads to the part it plays in narcissistic disorders and repetition compulsion, in fears of object loss and guilt, in defensive organizations which include idealization, self-aggrandizement, contempt and omnipotence.

Defences

Any study of envy is at the same time a study of the defences constructed against envy, and these defences are constructed not only because envy is an inherently painful emotion, nor because it is felt to be so reprehensible and guilt-inducing. The experience of envy is defended against because it is an acknowledgement of the otherness of the other, with all the terrifying consequences that arise from such an acknowledgement: foremost, dependence on an object who is not under one's control.

There is something particularly onerous about envy. Envious feelings – mental pain at the recognition that another person possesses something valuable – and the wish that this not be so – are experienced as bad and blameworthy, but also can create intolerable feelings of inferiority, humiliation and hatred. Because the experience of envy is so painful, it is powerfully defended against in many ways, and it is the defences we erect to prevent ourselves from feeling envious which are most pernicious. These defences always involve a destructive spoiling of the object; this spoiling can be predominantly in the mind of the subject, or it can be played out so that the object herself is attacked and her most enviable qualities spoilt. And there are different types of spoiling: spoiling can be denigrating and diminishing, or it can be over-valuing, idealizing. In either case, what is being spoiled is the recognition of the object's true, real qualities and real value. Furthermore, these attacks may be overt and even conscious, or they may be subtly undermining and more unconscious. While our picture of how this may work between a mother and her baby is largely theoretical, in an analysis we can watch how it works more closely and accurately and begin to have ways to address the process.

The phantasy of being eternally combined with the object is a self-protective defence against what can feel like overwhelming anxiety. When such a narcissistic phantasy is enduring, interfering with relations with real, important objects and overriding the perception of reality, it becomes characterological, what Rosenfeld (1971) called a *narcissistic organization* and Steiner (1993) has termed a *pathological organization*. Rosenfeld (1987) and Britton (2003) have written about the differences between those narcissistic disorders which are largely defensive (libidinal), and those which are largely destructive.

Triangularity

One of the most important issues in Klein's writing is that of triangularity. Klein herself explicitly refers to envy as being a two-person experience, differentiating it from jealousy, yet in an earlier paper she described at some length the infant's phantasies of its parents combined in an intercourse of continual oral, anal and genital satisfaction:

> oral frustration arouses in the child an unconscious knowledge that its parents enjoy mutual sexual pleasures and a belief at first that these are of an oral sort. Under the pressure of its own frustration, it reacts to this phantasy with envy of its parents ... an unconscious knowledge of this kind about sexual intercourse between the parents ... already emerges at the very early stage of development ... Oral envy ... soon cease(s) to be directed against the mother alone and become(s) extended to the father ... [and infants] imagine that his penis is incorporated by her during oral copulation and remains hidden inside her.
>
> (Klein, 1932, pp. 130–132)

And in 'Envy and Gratitude' she refers to envy being particularly stirred up during 'the earliest stages of the Oedipus complex' which includes the 'phantasies of the mother's breast and the mother containing the penis of the father ...' (Klein, 1957, p. 33).

The notion of the triangularity of the envious experience rests on the assumption that envy proper only emerges at a moment of differentiation: the gap in which separateness between self and object is momentarily perceived. It is this perception of separateness which creates the belief that the goodness of the object, now not belonging to the self, is being given to an Other, a third, even when this third is perceived to be other aspects of the self or the object.

Of course, even a very envious infant doesn't only envy his mother; he also, we have always to remember, deeply loves her since she is the embodiment of all the goodness that he knows. Indeed, his envy is a consequence of his experience of her as all the goodness in the world. And his sense of her as profoundly good, means that his envy and his hatred of her, and of her link with him, or with her own good internal objects, including his father's penis, creates powerful feelings of guilt in him. This is one of the vicious circles that Klein describes; the envious part of the self attacks the couple baby/mother, or patient/analyst, and this leads to a sense of guilt, a painful feeling of being bad and of being neither loving nor lovable. And this of course leads to despair about the self and then to such defences as persecution, or erotization. And as soon as the baby has a more realistic view of thinking, when father isn't present, father is experienced as being inside mother – inside her mind: the hatred is for the relationship of father in mother's mind.

What Is Gratitude?

Klein saw gratitude as the protector of loving feelings, opposing it to greed. Her argument is interesting; she saw greed as directed originally precisely towards the breast's specific contents: the milk that quells hunger. The appeasement of greed, Klein insisted, cannot bring gratification. It can bring satiation, a feeling of lack of hunger, an absence of appetite. But gratification, according to Klein, concerns experiences beyond the satisfaction of hunger: pleasure and delight from smell and from touch, from gazing and being gazed at, from being held comfortably and safely. It contains all the budding sensory and psychological experiences which will gradually become what we know as love. If greed can be understood to be about getting all the goodness for oneself – Klein links it with gorging and sucking out the content of the breast – then gratification can be seen to be about an experience of closeness and intimacy. And repeated experiences of gratification can lead to gratitude.

Gratitude is the acknowledgement, recognition and enjoyment that something good has been received – a 'gift'. Gratitude therefore requires an other; the gift is given me by an other. Gratitude proper arises at the moment of the gap – the moment it is recognized that the gift comes from another person, not from the self. At this moment, when hatred of the object – because it is other, because it is Not-Me – appears, gratitude is a mitigator of such hatred and a protector of loving feelings. Gratitude then is not just for a full belly, but for the multitude of experiences involved in the process of feeding and loving, being fed and loved: smelled, touched, held, gazed at. A benign cycle is opposed to the vicious cycle, creating a feeling of well-being; I am loved.

For Melanie Klein, it is gratitude that marks the movement from narcissism to object love and establishes it (as opposed to opposing it, denying it, obliterating it). Gratitude is the recognition and appreciation of otherness and is thus the marker of the capacity to internalize an object known to be separate from oneself.

It is a measure of Klein's lasting bequest that so much flows from 'Envy and Gratitude', a bountiful well from which any number of vessels can continue to be filled.

References

Bion, W. R. (1962) *Learning from Experience*. London: Heinemann.

Britton, R. (2003) *Sex, Death, and the Superego: Experiences in Psychoanalysis*. London: Routledge.

Klein, M. (1932) *The Psycho-analysis of Children*. London: Hogarth Press.

Klein, M. (1957) Envy and Gratitude. In M. Klein, *Envy and Gratitude and Other Works: 1946–1963* (pp. 176–235). London: Hogarth Press (1975).

Rosenfeld, H. (1971) A Clinical Approach to the Psychoanalytic Theory of the Life and Death Instincts: An Investigation into the Aggressive Aspects of Narcissism. *International Journal of Psychoanalysis* 52: 169–178.

Rosenfeld, H. (1987) *Impasse and Interpretation: Therapeutic and Anti-Therapeutic Factors in the Psychoanalytic Treatment of Psychotic, Borderline, and Neurotic Patients*. London: Routledge.

Steiner, J. (1993) *Psychic Retreats: Pathological Organizations in Psychotic, Neurotic and Borderline Patients*. London: Routledge.

Index

abandonment 19, 21, 32, 50, 52, 85, 104
abortion 42
Abraham, Karl 112, 116
aggression 37, 77
analysis: compared to relationship 67; dissatisfaction with 92; expectations of 81, 83–84, 91–92; integration and synthesis in 5; plan for ending 94–95
analyst: attacked by patient 51–52; contempt for 8, 53, 58, 59, 60; false 47; identification with 44, 47, 48; irritation with 72–73; need for strength 75; patients' feelings about 45; projection onto 52; rage at 51; relationship with 51, 54–58, 93–96, 114, 115
anxiety 26, 28, 31, 32, 55, 95; depressive 8, 45, 46, 88, 89; infantile 48; overwhelming 52, 65; persecutory 45, 64, 76; protection from 27
'as-if' personalities 3, 40, 43

Bion, Wilfred 48, 59, 99
boundary breaking 23
breast: attacking 76, 127; bad 65; full 72; good/ideal 4, 7, 64, 112, 123, 124; ideal 4, 7; inexhaustible 65, 122; mother's 122, 126, 127; of the patient 42–43; perfect 65; persecuting 4; relationship with 111, 122; and self-image 30; see also mother (analyst)
Britton, Ronald 126

chaos 109–110
child development 45–46; and the authentic self 109; and the ego 123; and idealization 65; paralysis of 77

childhood memories 20, 30, 36, 41, 42–43, 60–61, 66, 79, 97–98, 108, 120–121
Clinician's Guide to Reading Freud, A (Giovacchini) 13
countertransference 1, 29, 91
cruelty 2–3, 5, 7, 18, 25, 30, 31, 32, 33, 36, 37, 41, 75, 65, 75, 88, 94, 96, 97, 98, 103, 116

daydreams 98
death from despair 52
death instinct 122
denial 45; manic defence of 46
depression 2, 3, 5, 30, 36, 38, 40, 54, 79, 88, 104, 123; defences against 46; melancholic 50–51; transient 98
depressive anxiety 8, 45, 46, 88, 89
depressive position 1, 8, 45, 49, 51–52, 61, 65, 89, 105, 112; dream 5
Deutsch, Helene 3, 40, 53
disciplined curiosity 99
dis-integration 110
dreams: imaginary 114–115, 117; depressive position 5, 61; erotic 13; interpretation of 13–15, 21, 22–24, 43–44, 47, 48, 60–62, 97, 98, 99; levels of interpretation 15; omnipotent 72; psychic reality in 47; remembering 56; as response to real event 68, 71–72; *see also* phantasies

ego 3, 51, 52, 65, 109, 111, 122, 123; early 50; of the infant 45–46, 64; projection of parts from 27; rump- 112; *see also* projective identification
emotional landscape 25–26
empathy 4, 35, 40, 77

For Product Safety Concerns and Information please contact our EU
representative GPSR@taylorandfrancis.com
Taylor & Francis Verlag GmbH, Kaufingerstraße 24, 80331 München, Germany

www.ingramcontent.com/pod-product-compliance
Lightning Source LLC
Chambersburg PA
CBHW070346270326
41926CB00017B/4013

9 781032 959474